COMPLIMENTS OF

CITI

BANKER

TO THE

WORLD

BANKER
TO THE
WORLD

LEADERSHIP LESSONS
FROM THE FRONT LINES OF
GLOBAL FINANCE

WILLIAM R.
RHODES

NEW YORK   CHICAGO   SAN FRANCISCO
LISBON   LONDON   MADRID   MEXICO CITY   MILAN
NEW DELHI   SAN JUAN   SEOUL   SINGAPORE
SYDNEY   TORONTO

The **McGraw·Hill** Companies

1 2 3 4 5 6 7 8 9 0 DOC/DOC 1 6 5 4 3 2 1

ISBN 978-0-07-170425-0 (print book)
MHID   0-07-170425-6

ISBN 978-0-07-170424-3 (e-book)
MHID   0-07-170424-8

Library of Congress Cataloging-in-Publication Data

Rhodes, William R.
  Banker to the world : leadership lessons from the front lines of global finance / by William Rhodes.
     p. cm.
  ISBN 978-0-07-170425-0 (alk. paper)
  1. Rhodes, William R. 2. Bankers–United States–Biography. 3. Banks and banking, International. 4. International finance. 5. Leadership. 6. Decision making. I. Title.
  HG2463.R46.R46 2011
  332.1092–dc22
  [B]
                                                                    2010032040

McGraw-Hill books are available at special quantity discounts to use as premiums and sales promotions or for use in corporate training programs. To contact a representative, please e-mail us at bulksales@mcgraw-hill.com.

This book is printed on acid-free paper.

To the bankers, government officials, international financial institutions' staffs, and the lawyers who worked with me during the various debt crises of the 1980s and 1990s, and in particular to my colleagues at Citibank.

CONTENTS

CONTENTS

FOREWORD
BY PAUL A. VOLCKER

Bill Rhodes has for 50 years been a commercial banker, playing a prominent role in global finance. For some 30 of those years, our paths have been intertwined, he from the private sector, and I (most of the time) from the side of public policy. In fact, it is not too much to suggest that events forced us into a certain mutual dependency, a dependency growing out of our common concern about threats to the American—and the global—banking system.

The events first bringing us together have perhaps largely receded far into the background, partly forgotten by today's financial officials and market participants. Let me explain.

In the middle of 1982, financial markets were under strong pressure from recession, sky-high interest rates, and loan losses among commercial banks and, particularly, among savings institutions. Then, quite suddenly, what became known as the Latin American debt crisis hit market consciousness. Mexico was unable to pay its dollar debts to foreign banks—most important to U.S. banks, but also to almost all international bank lenders. Argentina,

Brazil, Venezuela, and Latin American and some Asian countries were not far behind. Altogether, the threatening losses would have deeply impaired the capital resources of international "money center" banks, foreign as well as American.

As chairman of the Federal Reserve at the time, I, along with administration colleagues, major foreign central banks, and especially the International Monetary Fund, could arrange stop-gap official financing and set out appropriate conditions for the heavily indebted borrower countries. But it was apparent from the start that the commercial banks themselves, with their own stability at risk, would need to stand together if they were to deal with the crisis, agree to a temporary standstill, and move quickly to organize joint and cooperative arrangements. Loans would need to be rolled over, maturities extended, and additional funds provided to support necessary reforms. No easy challenge for normally highly competitive banks asked to respond on short notice.

By some bit of serendipity, the right man appeared at the right time. Bill Rhodes was highly experienced in Latin America. As a senior official of Citibank, the largest and possibly the most exposed of the big banks, he knew both Latin American leaders and banking colleagues. It was natural that he be called upon to lead the rapidly formed committee of heavily exposed banks to deal with the Mexican crisis. As such, he was the main contact point for me and for the IMF.

What I didn't know then but soon learned was that Bill had the combination of qualities necessary not only to help the banks understand their common interest but also the compelling interests of the United States and those of other nations concerned with the threat to financial stability, the borrowing countries themselves, and international institutions. In some respects their perspectives were quite different, but there was a core of commonality that Bill comprehended well.

Within a few months, financial arrangements with the banks and the IMF were in place to backstop the first efforts of Mexico toward reform. Soon afterward Brazil found itself in deep trouble, and then others. Bill was involved in virtually every one of the rescue operations, drawing upon all his technical skill and diplomacy to establish confidence among the various parties, public and private.

What sticks in my mind to this day are the relatively ineffective efforts by other bankers who were called upon from time to time to lead the financing effort for particular countries. It was not that they lacked financial expertise. What was absent was an instinctive understanding of the varied interests at stake, the ability to marshal a consensus, and, when needed, the will to exert authority. Those were qualities Bill Rhodes brought to the table, and on more than one occasion I felt the need to implore Walter Wriston, then Citibank's chairman, to send Bill back into the fray.

That pattern has been repeated a number of times in the decades since I left office. The so-called Asian crisis in the 1980s is a leading case in point. The financial panic started with what was thought to be a limited devaluation of the Thai baht. Speculative pressures cascaded to Indonesia, to Malaysia, to elsewhere in South Asia, and eventually to South Korea. At a crucial point, efforts to contain and diffuse the crisis in South Korea, economically the largest and most advanced of the emerging Asian nations, seemed to be failing. Finally, Bill was urgently called to duty and promptly organized the needed standstill in trade credits. And somehow the tide turned.

That's only part of a consistent pattern. Bill Rhodes for decades has made a constructive contribution to international financial affairs. He has been a trusted advisor and confidant of most of our Treasury and central bank officials, starting at the top. That role has not been confined to the United States. Literally, two generations of leaders in the developing world economies and in the IMF have called upon him to explore ideas, and all have benefited from his insight. He became a strong voice in the leadership of the newly established Institute of International Finance, which has effectively improved research in emerging economies and coordinated efforts by financial institutions to strengthen risk-management practices.

Others can speak or write more fully of Bill's role within Citibank, particularly at times when the bank faced acute uncertainty. Of one thing I am certain: his internal responsibilities in managing risk, his extensive work with the official sector in the United States and elsewhere, and his willingness to speak out in public with words of warning, which, while entirely appropriate, could occasionally rub colleagues the wrong way. The last has never given Bill pause, even at perceived risks to his career.

The fact is that Bill could, by instinct, by education, and by experience, bridge the worlds of private finance and public responsibility with benefit to both. That is a quality that too few possess. Longtime public servants (i.e., bureaucrats) often fail to recognize the market opportunities, the need to innovate, and the competitive requirements for success in business and finance. Those accustomed to and successful in business (i.e., capitalists) typically find it equally difficult to accommodate to the pressures and requirements of public life, political and administrative, where there is no clear bottom line, but rather need to achieve consensus and to ensure fair and consistent treatment in the general interest.

Banker to the World, with its Lessons for Leadership, distills in flowing prose what Bill Rhodes has learned over the decades in the front line of global finance. In its mechanics, in its enormous complexity, in its now engrained international character, the world of banking has changed radically from those days a generation ago when I first met Bill. What hasn't changed in dealing with crises is the need for some basic qualities of leadership, qualities that Bill has personified: vision, a combination of skill and drive to implement that vision, the ability to build consensus even among those from different cultures and with competing interests, and a refusal to be intimidated and to back down from what is fair and right.

Through it all, one quality stands out from my experience in working with Bill Rhodes and observing him in action.

Tenacity, stick-to-itiveness, get it done!

These days it has become rare to spend 50 years in one institution, sticking with it through its downs as well as ups. *Banker to the World* is testimony to the simple fact that one man could find enormous satisfaction in that kind of career, extending his reach beyond the private institution to the challenges of the world that affect all institutions, public and private alike.

Bill Rhodes takes on responsibility. He stays with it. In the process he has served his bank, his country, and the world of finance with remarkable courage and great distinction.

I, for one, am glad he put pen to paper to describe that career—mindful there are still chapters that lie ahead.

ACKNOWLEDGMENTS

Through the years a number of people suggested that I put down my thoughts on my experiences in international finance, and particularly in crisis prevention and crisis management, as a guide for future generations. Unfortunately my pressing business schedule has not permitted me to firm up these thoughts in writing until now.

This book could not have been written without the support of Sheridan Prasso, whom I would like to thank for her ideas, guidance, and patience.

I would also like to single out Cecilia Bartner, the late Antro Sarkissian, and Marysue Farley, on whose generous collaboration I could always rely. Their suggestions were valuable and appreciated. Special mention also goes to Dick Howe, to whom I owe a debt of gratitude for his support over the years and his meaningful input to this book.

I would be remiss if I did not offer my thanks to Paul Volcker, who kindly supplied the Foreword to the book and who has been a good friend and supporter for many years, and to Bob Dineen, my trusted advisor, who provided thoughtful commentary along the way.

Research for the book permitted me to contact friends I had not seen or spoken to in several years. Talking to them to refresh my memory and reminisce about our shared experiences was an added bonus to this process. I would like to express my appreciation to friends and colleagues who made themselves available to read the manuscript in whole or in part, at times more than once, and who provided good advice and suggestions, in particular to Dick Aldrich, Rima Ayas, Andrea Bauer, Jorge Bermudez, Chris Brougham, Kathryn Carassalini, Terry Checki, David Coulter, Charles Dallara, Mike de Graffenried, Jacques de Larosière, Kemal Dervis, Carlos Fedrigotti, Helene Freeman, Arminio Fraga, Carlos Guimaraes, Jim Hammond, Mike Hunter, Guy Huntrods, Dick Handley, Tom Jones, Michael Katzke, T.C. Koo, Jacquie Kouyoumjian, Edgard Leal, Alan MacDonald, David Martin, John Millard, Jeanne Olivier, Jeff Shafer, Carlos Steneri, Rick Suarez, Jose Taboada, and Frank and Emily Vogl.

My appreciation to my loyal and competent support staff over the years: Carmen Net, the late Alma Padron, Pablo Hidalgo, and Paula Wong.

I was very fortunate to have McGraw-Hill as my publisher. Its staff, and in particular Leah Spiro, my first editor; Mary Glenn, the associate publisher, business and finance; and Janice Race, the senior editing supervisor, were instrumental in ensuring that I finish the book. I am grateful to them and to the people at McGraw-Hill who worked so hard at making this book a reality.

I am grateful to Ram Charan and Jane Ren who encouraged me to write the book early on, along with many other people who are too numerous to mention, and to Louise Tilzer for her help with the book cover.

And last but not least, to my daughter, Elizabeth; my sister, Nancy; and my brother-in-law, Dick, I offer my thanks for their continuous support and for their love.

INTRODUCTION

The great Chinese military tactician Sun Tzu once wrote, "The quality of a decision is like the well-timed swoop of a falcon." In the realm of international banking, where I have spent more than five decades of my career, I have had to swoop into difficult situations over and over again.

My mission has always been to build—to help developing economies repay their staggering debts, to restore their access to credit markets, and to help them return to growth and obtain access to new markets. I have tried to act with falconlike precision to warn institutions, and not just my own, of impending crises so that they could act to stave off the repercussions. Also, I have always worked to take advantage of opportunities to expand financial services throughout the world.

All of these situations, both at home and abroad, have taught me many lessons. And it is these lessons, along with the traits and qualities that I have developed over these many years, that I now seek to pass on to others.

The following chapters explore these lessons through a series of anecdotes—experiences from my career that illustrate key themes that I would like to impart. The trials and errors, and the successes and failures along the way, collectively provide a path of instruction for those both in the international financial community and outside it.

It is important to note that these lessons are not relevant just for bankers, managers, or investors; they apply to a whole host of situations in any number of contexts. For example, negotiating situations are the same the world over, whether or not they have to do with debt restructuring.

The common theme of all of them can be summed up with one of my favorite expressions: *tempus fugit,* the Latin for "time flies." In a crisis, the clock is always working against you. Time is your enemy. Sometimes a crisis takes a long time to build, but when it hits, its impact is instantaneous and immediate. Therefore, crises, be they economic, political, or both, require decisive time management. They require planning and communication. They require immediate action. In a crisis, you must make decisions quickly, communicate them clearly, and implement them rapidly. You must have a credible plan and communicate it immediately. You must have the conviction of the correctness of your actions, and work persistently and tirelessly to implement them. In fact, for all the lessons stated here, there was a key time and place for the actions taken, which is perhaps the most relevant lesson of all. As the Book of Ecclesiastes in the Bible states, there is a time and a purpose for everything:

> A time to sow and a time to reap, . . .
> a time to tear down and a time to build, . . .
> a time to search and a time to give up, . . .
> a time to tear and a time to mend, a time to be silent
>   and a time to speak.

I think about these verses every time I take action. It is by knowing when and how to act—which time is for which purpose—that we can be most effective.

Another tendency that has served me well has been sheer tenacity, which comes through in so many of the lessons here. Over the years, nothing in my career has been truer than the philosophy that persistence pays. In countless late-night-into-early-morning negotiations to restructure the debts of Mexico, Brazil, Uruguay, Peru, South Korea, and many other countries, I became well known for carrying on negotiations, refusing to break for sleep, until we came to a consensus. I knew well that at 4 a.m., the term to which a holdout participant has been so strenuously objecting suddenly becomes more palatable. At the same time, I always knew that it was important in negotiations to concede just enough that everyone felt that he or she came away from the table with at least a small victory. This is my counsel to those who would follow in similar situations. Recognize when persistence will result in a breakthrough, and stick with it unflaggingly until you get one.

In part, knowing what to do and when to act comes down to character. I believe that character is formed at a young age, but is developed and enriched with each new experience. One of the reasons for my love of history, which has served me well in countless meetings with international officials over the years, is my father, Edward Reginald, who was known as Reg. He was very much an internationalist. He had been the youngest Marine Corps major in World War I. During World War II, he rejoined the service, this time in the army, which asked him to become part of a planning group for the North African campaign. In that capacity, he led an Allied battalion of combat engineers that landed in Oran during the invasion of North Africa, which culminated in the defeat of the German Afrika Korps.

We discussed history and international affairs at the dinner table at our home on Long Island when I was a boy. My father traveled all over the world for Standard Oil of California as a first mate and then as captain on oil tankers, going to places such as China and Brazil, among others. He worked for Royal Dutch Shell and Shell-Mex in Mexico, Venezuela, and the Dutch West Indies (before it came to be called Netherlands Antilles).

And he loved military history. On a radio show broadcast on WINS in New York, where he was a military commentator before the U.S. entrance into World War II, he predicted almost to the day—February 15, 1942—the fall of Singapore to Japanese troops. The commander of the major British base in the Pacific, Lieutenant General A. E. Percival, had believed that the Japanese would invade the island by sea, but instead the Japanese advanced down the Malay Peninsula and found the garrison inadequately defended from the rear—just as my father had foretold.

As a result of these enthralling discussions, I would often stay up late with a flashlight, reading history books in bed, until my parents came in and told me to go to sleep. To this day, I am still an avid reader of military history, and of history in general.

When I was a freshman at Brown University, of course majoring in history, I decided that I wanted to see the world for myself. I got my seaman's papers and determined to work on a ship sailing around the world, which I did in the summers after my freshman and sophomore years. I couldn't get on a U.S. ship, so I found Danish freighters that would take me. In order to survive on a ship full of Danes, Norwegians, Swedes, Spaniards, and men of other nationalities, I had to learn to get along with people—their customs, their mores, and how they operated in close quarters. In a situation like that, you grow to respect people no matter who they are or where they come from.

One year my bunkmate was a Spaniard, from Spanish Morocco, so I practiced my Spanish with him. We sailed through the Panama Canal and down the coast of South America, one year down the east coast and another year down the west coast. I gained fluency in the language in the ports of call, in Panama, Chile, Peru, Colombia, Argentina, and Uruguay. I learned some Portuguese in Brazil as well. These experiences have served my career in ways that I could not have imagined at the time. As a result, my recommendation that people who are working in foreign countries take the time to learn the language and get to know the people is one of the key lessons of this book.

I didn't set out intending to be a banker. I had busted up my knee playing lacrosse just before graduation, so I couldn't go into the military, which was what I had planned to do. I needed a job, and it was a recession year. I was lucky to be able to get a job interview with George Moore at First National City Bank of New York (renamed Citibank in 1976), who was then the executive vice president for overseas operations and who would later become chairman.

"Are you a worker?" Moore asked me. "We have plenty of talkers in this bank, but what we need are workers."

Obviously, I said yes. I needed the job. Because of my Spanish-language ability, I was assigned to the East Caribbean desk in New York and was soon dispatched to Venezuela. It turned out that I liked banking and wanted to make a career of it.

Those of us who worked in Latin America between the 1950s and the 1970s remember the political unrest, military governments, and economic models that favored closed markets and heavy public-sector involvement. Venezuela, as a Latin American democracy, was the site that President Kennedy chose to initiate his Alliance for Progress, a program of aid and development aimed at improving U.S. relations with Latin America. I remember that event well: I was a young Citibank branch officer in Venezuela in those days, and I was asked to be among the group that would greet JFK at the airport in Caracas.

It was a hot, tense occasion. Guerrillas backed by Cuba's Fidel Castro had broadcast threats against Kennedy's life. Huge crowds, hoping for a glimpse of the president, lined the roads, and the sun reflected off the bayonets of nervous soldiers cordoning the airfield. When Air Force One landed, Kennedy announced that he had arrived in the footsteps of Franklin Delano Roosevelt, who had declared that the United States was dedicated to a "policy of the good neighbor" toward Latin America. I felt a surge of pride that has stayed with me my entire life. Later, when he vowed, through the alliance, "to make all our hemisphere a bright and shining light over all the world," our hopes were high.

Yet the economic model that most Latin American countries chose to follow in those years proved faulty. What appeared to be promising economic growth in the late 1960s and early 1970s gave way to bloated and inefficient public sectors, highly protected industries, a dearth of private enterprises, and huge debts incurred principally by public-sector companies. As a result, when faced with high interest rates and a global recession at the beginning of the next decade, many countries were unable to repay their international obligations, producing the debilitating debt crisis of the 1980s.

We worked hard to get Latin America through that dark period, but it was the people of Latin America and their governments who finally recognized the need for basic structural economic reforms. Dedicated leaders in many Latin American countries endeavored to restructure their debt, privatize industries, build institutions, and open their markets to the free movement of money and goods, as we will see in the lessons that follow.

The result is that capital flows today are directed mainly toward the private sector, with a new emphasis on equity rather than debt. Modern technology, better management, and the creation and expansion of local capital markets are guiding these new capital flows toward more productive uses. Capital is now allocated to investment in plants and equipment rather than financing deficits, and investors today are afforded additional protection through improved transparency in accounting rules and disclosure requirements. However, as the events of 2008–2009 showed, there is still an urgent need for international accounting standards and regulatory reforms.

In Latin America during the 1980s, a significant change in governance practices occurred, as many capitals went from military governments to democracies. At the same time, there was a massive opening up of the economies to structural economic reform and privatization.

Reform does not happen overnight. Countries need time, both to implement the structural adjustments that are necessary for reform and to sort through the inevitable failures associated with such a tremendous undertaking.

The adjustments to these countries' debt obligations that we undertook—and that are the subject of so many of the lessons here—bought them time. Yet in several cases, Latin American countries have been backsliding. Only the future will reveal whether these lessons will remain absorbed in the countries in which they have taken hold, and how permanently and broadly economic reform will spread in the rest of the region.

Still, all who went through the crises of the 1980s and 1990s can take some pride in what was accomplished. The process of resolving the debt crises has benefited both the countries and their creditors alike. In retrospect, though, in some cases the reform measures were probably overly austere and imposed undue hardships on the countries' citizens. The lessons learned here should be taken into account for future economic reform packages supported by the IMF and the World Bank.

During the early years of the foreign debt crisis, some experts suggested that a cookie-cutter solution could be applied to every country. But it soon became apparent that each country was unique. From country to country, economic policies, by necessity, reflected the differing realities of the countries themselves. Over and over again, I urged borrowers and lenders alike to understand the need for individual solutions in order to help both debtors and creditors maximize their recoveries. I largely succeeded.

In the early 1980s, securitization was very different from the mechanisms and products used today, where the secondary markets for developing-country debt are among the more enduring legacies of international debt crises. Liquidity has added considerable value.

The first step toward securitization of the foreign debt came in 1984, when Mexico and its creditor banks agreed, as part of a multiyear restructuring, to allow the conversion of Mexican debt into equity. Chile, Argentina, and other countries later used this restructuring instrument in their privatization efforts. This innovation, which my colleagues and I helped to implement, heralded a market-based solution to the recurring debt problems of the developing world. The main idea was that all participants should accept the use of market solutions to encourage and retain voluntary flows of private capital. In a market environment, confidence is the name of the game.

In the succeeding years, the market for Latin American and developing-country debt developed into a global market, with annual turnover of more than half a trillion dollars by the mid-1990s. Today, it is no longer the commercial banks that hold the majority of emerging-market debt. It is held by ordinary investors and institutions in the form of mutual funds, hedge funds, and pension funds.

This new financial architecture required efforts to prevent new crises from developing. I urged that financial firms improve their risk-management practices and integrate their country analysis and risk-measurement systems more closely to avoid unsound lending. Unfortunately, these processes, which Citi called "Windows on Risk," did not carry over past the late 1990s.

I learned early on that in a crisis, it is important not to cut and run. During various foreign debt crises over the years, I watched as many lenders closed offices and sold off loans at a loss to put the problems behind them. But when the debtors' economies recovered again, many of the same institutions were clamoring to get back in. The temptation to wipe the slate clean was keenly felt when the market battered bank stocks that had high nonperforming-loan ratios.

I always warned lenders to resist the temptation to sell prematurely, and I advocate the same today. At the same time, I urged them not to be afraid to deal in the marketplace. That meant that they should first apply objective analysis to the decision about how and when to dispose of assets, whether performing or nonperforming, including those that had been acquired by default. Clearly, time and time again, economic and market trends were not accurately assessed when the initial financing and investment decisions were being made. When owners performed an analysis of the time value of money—particularly as it pertained to the real estate market over the years—they often found that extra time afforded them the opportunity to find buyers, lessening the impulse to cut and run. These lessons have strong parallels to the situation that the world finds itself in today.

Flawed analyses should be recognized and not repeated. In most cases, those who stay in for the long haul stand a better chance of realizing the full value of their assets. They will be in the best position to profit when the market recovers.

Much of my career was spent managing through crises, which required a study of the underlying causes and drivers of the problems. This led naturally to a focus on crisis prevention, and although in some cases my advice was heeded, in other cases it was ignored. For example, beginning in 2005, I was among the first to see the warning signs that rocky times were on the horizon. A column titled "The Curse of

Cheap Credit?" by Robert J. Samuelson in the *Washington Post* on June 2, 2005, quoted me as saying that we were on our way to a repeat of past crises: "The speculation here is more evident than people seem to realize." What I meant, of course, was that early on, it was apparent to me that cheap credit was accumulating too quickly and that eventually the economy would face its reckoning. The *Wall Street Journal* quoted me in another article on June 16, 2005, as expressing concern about a growing housing bubble. "Lenders and investors have to be careful that they exercise proper risk management," I said. "If they don't, they're going to get burned."

Then, in April 2006, while attending a meeting of the Inter-American Development Bank in Brazil and after discussions with reporters there, I was quoted in the *Financial Times* as urging the world's biggest financial institutions to be "very careful." I noted the size of the U.S. current-account and fiscal deficits, and the possibility of slower growth in emerging markets. "The days of easy money are over," I said. "We are in a situation similar to that which existed in the spring of 1997 when threats existed to market stability and a lot of people didn't want to see it. I am not predicting a new Asia crisis, but it is interesting to see the similarities that are present. There is a need for lenders and investors to be prudent."

I warned of impending crisis again in an op-ed in the *Financial Times* on March 29, 2007. It was titled "A Market Correction Is Coming, This Time for Real." I said that periods of economic expansion tend to last between five and seven years, and that we were entering the sixth year of expansion, which would make 2008 the seventh. I wrote:

Pockets of excess are becoming harder to ignore. Problems in the housing and mortgage area such as the sub-prime sector in the U.S. are one such example of excess that should come as no surprise. As lenders and investors inevitably become more discriminating, liquidity will recede and a number of problems will surface.

I ended with a prediction. "What is clear to me is that in the next year, a material correction in the markets will occur," I insisted. "This is clearly the time to exercise greater prudence in lending and to resist any temptation to relax standards." These comments were widely read around the world, having been picked up by other publications.

Shortly after this, I was invited by the CEO of Scotiabank, Rick Waugh, to address his board of directors at their annual off-site meeting. I handed out copies of my op-ed and proceeded to reiterate my position: that a big market correction was coming. I am told that my concerns about the economic vulnerabilities of the market caught their attention and impressed on them the need for caution in their risk-management activities.

Most of the banking community didn't think that a correction was coming that quickly. Their rationale was that it took a while for Japan's bubble to burst, so they didn't think the one in the U.S. market would collapse so fast. They thought they had more time.

I was called a Cassandra by many in the press and in the news. But the lesson here is that it's better to be right early than to be wrong later.

While in some cases I warned of coming crises and was listened to, other times I was not.

What is clear is that financial institutions need to do a much better job of risk management and corporate governance. And regulators need to do a better job of regulatory oversight. We need sound, smart, and realistic regulation that is implemented on a continual basis, to ensure that risks are managed appropriately, yet innovation is not stifled.

As institutions go about fixing these problems, they find that they are also changing business fundamentals in a positive way. In a very real sense, they're creating a future from the wreckage of the past.

The first lesson that follows in the pages ahead, regarding the need for bold leadership, requires decisions that can be implemented in any context, from the conference table to the world beyond.

The same broad applicability pertains to the need for vision (Lesson 2); to the ability to execute in a timely fashion (Lesson 3); to the need for prompt, proactive, and comprehensive action (Lesson 4); and to the importance of standing up for what is right (Lesson 5). Most of the stories that exemplify these lessons have elements of the other lessons, too, or else the outcomes would not have been successful.

In reflecting upon a lifelong career, it is just as important to recount one's failures as to recount one's successes. It was John F. Kennedy, then a candidate for president, who introduced a new word into the American lexicon in a speech in April 1959. The word was *weiji*, and it is central to Lesson 6.

> When written in Chinese, the word *crisis* is composed of two characters. One represents danger, and the other represents opportunity.

Pronounced "way-GEE," this word is a handy tool, a call to action for those who are sitting on the sidelines, unable to understand that nowhere is the opportunity to act more promising than in a crisis. Acting on opportunity is clearly a success. But not seizing opportunity is a failure. This has been the case over and over in my career. Citibank's branch openings throughout Eastern Europe are good examples of seizing opportunities in a positive fashion.

Over the years, I have been able to use my love of international affairs, of foreign languages, and of history to good effect. In Lesson 7, I show how in numerous discussions with Chinese officials, it was my keen interest in and knowledge of Chinese culture and history that helped me to secure Citibank's access to new markets in China. In Venezuela, my knowledge of the language, the history, and the culture prevented Citibank from being nationalized in the 1970s.

Finally, the consensus-building techniques that I employed with the committees I chaired to work out South Korea's and the Latin American countries' debt payments— elaborated on in Lesson 8—are universal. For me, those techniques were critical in resolving issues at board meetings at Northfield Mount Hermon School in western Massachusetts, the prep school I attended as a teenager and for which I served as the board chair as an adult. I have employed the same methods while serving as chairman of various other boards, such as the Council of the Americas, the Americas Society, the U.S.-Hong Kong Business Council, and the U.S.-Korea Business Council; as first vice chair of the Institute of International Finance; and as president of the Bankers' Association for Finance and Trade and the Venezuelan American Chamber of Commerce, among others.

The world is a far different place from what it was back in 1957, when I began my career with Citibank. We have been through the oil shocks of the 1970s; the recessions of the 1980s and early 1990s; the end of the cold war, which fundamentally changed the dynamics of global finance; and now the Great Recession. We currently operate with the primacy of capitalism as our economic driver, rather than a bifurcated system that hindered global development. Yet as we have seen from the events that gave the world a financial shock in 2008 and the challenge to the euro precipitated by Greece's troubles in 2010, the potential for crisis has not abated. The new sets of challenges may seem different, but in fact they are similar. They require the kinds of bold leadership, decisive action, and tenacity that I have lived by for more than five decades as a global banker and that are described in this book.

LEAD BOLDLY AND DECISIVELY

Facing Down the Sandinistas of Nicaragua,
The Middle East and Israel,
and Getting the Deal Done in China

B old decision making is the hallmark of leading in cri-sis situations, and it is a skill that I have had to employ time and again over my 50-year career. In a time of crisis, it is important to recognize the course of action that needs to be taken, and to take that action quickly. The following three examples are cases in which, when faced with chal-lenges, taking bold decisions resulted in positive outcomes.

In Nicaragua in 1980, for example, I had to insist that gun-toting Sandinistas not disrupt our debt negotiations—and was rewarded with a box of cigars from Fidel Castro follow-ing the deal's completion. In the early 1990s, I overrode the concerns of some of my colleagues, who were worried about Citibank's position in the Middle East, in order to open a Citibank presence in Israel in the spirit of the Oslo Accords. And in China, I led Citibank through the acquisition of a stake in a local bank that required a decision on my part to go ahead and take responsibility for signing the deal, de-spite eleventh-hour problems at the signing ceremony.

The lessons illustrated here demonstrate that when faced with challenges, adversity, skeptics, last-minute snafus—and even armed guards—leadership in these types of situations requires making a bold decision about a course of action and then motivating the teams around you to carry that decision through. To lead, you must be proactive and courageous—and willing to take the responsibility if your measures fail.

NICARAGUA

I had spent 20 years working in Latin America and the Caribbean before I was faced with Daniel Ortega and his submachine-gun–toting Sandinistas. I will never forget that experience, and it is an example of the type of leadership that I advocate for anyone who is in a position to lead people and shape outcomes: engaging in bold, direct action; making clear decisions; and then sticking to those decisions without wavering or backing down.

On July 19, 1979, Ortega and his comandantes seized power in Nicaragua. They inherited a national debt of $1.6 billion, including $582 million owed to 115 private banks around the world. We at Citi were one of those banks, and we had a branch in downtown Managua. As a senior vice president in charge of corporate banking in Latin America, I decided to fly down to assess the situation.

The Sandinistas—a new, leftist government that had just taken over from a long-running conservative regime—had been in power just three weeks, and the mood was tense. As our Falcon 20 taxied to a stop at the airport in Managua, we were met by a number of female fatigue-clad soldiers carrying AK-47s. They were to be my escorts for my few-hour visit to the city. I was to fly out the same day, under threat of execution right there on the tarmac if we did not leave on time.

"Your plane will leave on time because otherwise my leader has given me orders to shoot you," one of the Sandinista women said to me by way of greeting upon arrival.

She said the same to our pilot.

I assured her in Spanish that we would be leaving exactly as scheduled. But I would have preferred a slightly more friendly welcome. It happened to be my forty-fourth birthday—August 15, 1979. When it came to the Sandinistas, I didn't have a philosophical bent.

On the way into the city, I could see streets pockmarked by the remnants of heavy fighting. Several years of Sandinista rebellion and the regime's attempts to quell it had left 50,000 people, or 2 percent of the population, dead. For more than a year, National Guard troops had used artillery and aerial bombs to devastate the eastern part of the city while trying to rout the Sandinista rebels, demolishing schools, hospitals, and vital electric and water infrastructure, and killing thousands in Managua alone.

On top of the manmade destruction, the 1972 earthquake had also wreaked terrible devastation on Managua—80 percent of the buildings had been destroyed, and the city center had been reduced to rubble. Seven years later, there was no sign of rebuilding and little evidence of the massive amounts of aid that had poured into the country for reconstruction. The downtown streets were mostly empty save for ruins, and roads led out of town through wastelands to hastily built shantytowns on the perimeter. The toppled president, Anastasio (Tachito) Somoza

Debayle—the younger son of Nicaragua's original dictator, who had been assassinated in 1956—had appointed himself head of the earthquake reconstruction committee and had awarded his own companies 80 percent of the building contracts; however, only a fraction of these were ever completed. Downtown Managua was virtually abandoned, as most of the rebuilding that had been done had taken place on land in the south and southeast of the city, which had been owned by Somoza and his associates.

Like most businesses in Managua, our bank branch was closed. As I had requested, I was taken to meet Arturo Cruz, Sr., the head of the Central Bank. Cruz, who had a degree from Georgetown University, had long been working to overthrow the Somoza regime. He had been jailed twice, once following a failed plot in 1947 and again following another such plot in 1954. He had gone into exile in Washington to work for the Inter-American Development Bank, where I had met him. During that period, the FSLN (*Frente Sandinista de Liberación Nacional*) had approached him and enlisted his support.

When the Sandinistas succeeded in toppling the Somoza regime, Cruz returned to head the Central Bank in Managua—but not before transferring control of the Nicaraguan embassy in Washington to the new Sandinista government. Cruz and some of his associates took up quarters downstairs and left the outgoing Somoza ambassador to settle his affairs on the second floor. (Cruz resigned from the Central Bank post in 1981 to become ambassador to the United States, and he ultimately joined the Contras in 1985 before quitting them as well two years later.) These Sandinistas considered themselves elitists, not guerrillas, and their intent was to bring a new leftist order to Nicaragua that would erase the injustices of the Somoza years for the benefit of the Nicaraguan people.

Cruz assured me during our meeting that Nicaragua was committed to restructuring its international debt obligations. I was pleased to hear it, and so I returned to New York with the good news that the Sandinista government would support debt restructuring talks.

But just a month later, at a speech to the General Assembly of the United Nations in September, Daniel Ortega raised alarms in the international banking community.

"Nicaragua's foreign debt should be assumed by the international community, especially the developed countries and above all those who supported the Somoza regime," he said. This raised fears that the Nicaraguans would do what Fidel Castro had done in Cuba—nationalize U.S. banks and selectively repudiate most of his foreign debt. The Mexicans stepped in to mediate and offered to host debt negotiations in Mexico City. Clearly there were divisions emerging among those who headed the new ruling junta. It seemed that there would only be a short window in which to negotiate.

The Nicaraguan side was led by a young man named Alfredo César Aguirre, just 28 years old. He had studied industrial relations at the University of Texas, so his English was fluent, and he had been a spokesman for the Sandinista movement in New York as well, which meant that he was used to the wheeling-dealing ways of Manhattan. (He later replaced Cruz at the Central Bank and then followed him into the Contra camp as well.) He would be a formidable negotiating counterpart.

In the interim, in December 1979, the Council of the Americas, a U.S.-based business organization made up of private-sector business leaders who were interested in fostering economic development and democracy in the Western Hemisphere, invited three of Nicaragua's new leaders to New York. Some of the members of the board, including myself, took them to see *Evita* at the Broadway Theater in Times Square. Starring the fantastic Patti LuPone playing Argentina's tragic leader Eva Perón, the musical had opened just a few months before to rave reviews. As the ticketholders took their seats, they all marched in—the three comandantes dressed in fatigues, accompanied by their female "secretaries," also in fatigues. When the Che Guevara character came out on stage, everyone in the theater thought it was a put-on, what with these comandantes in the audience. I had my own "comandante" credentials as well: in those days they used to call me Comandante Gucci, for the loafers with the buckle on the front that I used to wear.

I didn't chair the first two Nicaraguan sessions in Mexico, and those meetings were largely procedural. But by the time we got down to business, to hear the proposals and counterproposals from both sides, I had been asked to head the committee that would be in charge of working out a restructuring plan on behalf of those 115 banks from several dozen countries. My job was to get back the $582 million owed to the banks.

Our first real negotiations took place March 19, 1980, in Managua. I had flown down again—this time without the threat of execution if I overstayed my welcome—and checked into the InterContinental Hotel, which was the only functioning hotel of international standards at that time. The hotel had a jogging route around the hill it was perched upon, and, as an avid runner, I went out early in the morning before negotiations started. As it happened, I injured my Achilles tendon, so it hurt to walk into the meeting room. It was a bad omen: the Sandinistas showed up flanked by guards armed with AK-47s, the type of submachine guns they had first threatened me with at the airport on my visit seven months before.

The Nicaraguans evidently thought that they could get more out of us by scaring us. Yet I refused to negotiate under the threat of force. I insisted that the Sandinistas who were standing at the doors, with their weapons at the ready, be made to exit the room or I would break off negotiations immediately. They complied, but the negotiations over the following three days were tense, held under the threat of the armed soldiers just outside the doors. On the agenda was the first $490 million owed to more than 100 foreign banks.

In order to put our discussions on an even playing field, I had to find neutral territory. I decided on Panama—the Holiday Inn in Panama City. A lot of banks in Latin America, including Citi, ran their Central American operations out of there. It was also easy for the Nicaraguans to travel to. After one more meeting in Mexico in April, that's where we held the final rounds of talks.

The talks were still continuing when the one-year anniversary of the revolution was approaching in July 1980. I returned to Managua on a U.S. government plane that took off from Andrews Air Force Base, representing the private sector as part of an official U.S. delegation. It was led by the U.S. ambassador to the United Nations, Donald McHenry, and included the attorney general for the state of New Mexico, who was a Spanish speaker. President

Jimmy Carter was sending us down for the celebrations. He was concerned that Nicaragua would go the way of Cuba, falling into the Soviet orbit in the midst of the cold war. Washington needed to keep up relations, and Carter hoped that he could lure the Sandinistas into the U.S. sphere of influence despite the munitions and support that they had received from Castro. He had authorized a modest assistance package to help the new government. This was, of course, before President Reagan came into office, named Nicaragua one of five countries making up a "confederation of terrorist states" (along with Libya, Cuba, North Korea, and Iran), and authorized the CIA to begin financing for the group that would become the Contras.

It was boiling hot in Managua—over 100 degrees—and people were collapsing from the heat. The longest speech that day was, of course, by Fidel Castro, whose government had allied with the Sandinistas in their overthrow of the Somoza regime and was providing military and technical assistance to the new government. Ortega spoke seemingly as long.

Daniel Ortega—who in 2007 was once again elected president—wanted my help to do him a favor: would I speak with Castro in an effort to improve Cuba's relations with the international financial community?

So we sat down for coffee and his Cuban Cohiba cigars, just Fidel and me, for an hour-long meeting. Cohibas were his preferred cigar, so it was an indulgence to smoke one with him. He told me that he had made a mistake in putting in Che Guevara as governor of Cuba's Central Bank. The old joke going around Latin American circles at the time, which some insisted was true, was that when Fidel assembled his men in the aftermath of the takeover of

Havana and said, "Who here is an *economista?*" Guevara misunderstood the question and thought Castro had asked, "Who here is a *comunista?*" Che raised his hand.

Castro wanted advice on how to restructure Cuba's foreign debt. He also said that he had made a mistake by leaving the International Monetary Fund, the World Bank, and the Inter-American Development Bank, and that he had warned Ortega not to follow the same route so as not to cut himself off from international funding.

But what could Cuba do now? U.S. banks had been nationalized when Fidel took power, but Cuba still owed outstanding debts to Canadian and European banks—mainly Spanish ones. The Soviets weren't going to help. He needed debt relief, which is when banks agree to forgive or restructure debt, similar to when a credit card borrower negotiates for lower payments.

I advised Castro that he had to go about it in an organized manner, with representatives of the banks involved, in order to ensure the country's reputation in international capital markets. It was then that Castro bet me that I wouldn't be able to pull off a restructuring deal for the Nicaraguans any time soon. He gave a date.

I bet him that I would.

He said that if I succeeded, he would send me a box of Cohibas, his personal cigars.

Later that year, we finalized the deal with the Nicaraguans. One night, after months of tense negotiations that debated not just principal and interest rates, but also principles and ideology, we had a breakthrough. Everyone assembled in the suite of our head of Central American operations, who was temporarily working out of Panama because of an ongoing civil war in Guatemala, and was snarling and cranky after a long day. For comic relief, the representative from Merrill Lynch began telling jokes. Everyone started to laugh. When we finally stopped, someone said, "Hey, this is the deal we have on the table. Let's just do it." So the tired group reached agreement right there. The deal was done.

For the first time in any rescheduling in recent memory, we agreed to defer both interest and principal payments on the $582 million and to stretch out the repayment of interest and principal over a 12-year period. Normally, a rescheduling period would be 7 years. At the signing ceremony in Panama City, the Nicaraguans signed the agreement with a gold Cross pen that their lawyer had embossed with the words:

Firmar me harás
Pagar jamás

This means: "You can make me sign, but you'll never make me pay." It ultimately turned out to be true—the Nicaraguans subsequently did not live up to their agreement. After the signing that evening, however, they celebrated heartily by smoking cigars.

On that occasion, I was reminded of Fidel's promise. But I never heard from him.

Until years later. In February 1986, an article titled "Field Marshal of the Debt Crisis" appeared in *Institutional Investor* magazine. In recounting my dealings with the Nicaraguans as well as other workouts that I had engineered after that time in other countries of Latin America, the article mentioned Fidel's bet.

A month later, I received a call from Cuba's ambassador to the United Nations. He had a box of Cohibas to deliver to me, courtesy of Fidel Castro. He made an appointment to see me in my fifth-floor office on Park Avenue. I asked my lawyer, John Millard, who had been my lawyer in the negotiations and spoke fluent Spanish, to sit in. I didn't know what to expect. When the ambassador arrived, accompanied by an assistant who I was sure was an intelligence agent, he was carrying the cigars under his arm. As he handed them to me, the ambassador said confidently, "Fidel always keeps his word."

In a sense, this box of cigars represented a kind of recognition for the boldness to take a leadership role in trying to bring Nicaragua back into the international banking fold and for standing up against armed Sandinista guards and insisting on a neutral negotiating atmosphere.

THE MIDDLE EAST AND ISRAEL

Sometimes you have to make a bold decision that goes against all advice—with the conviction that it is the right thing to do and the hope that all will work out in the end.

The story begins on October 31, 1994, when I attended the Casablanca Summit, otherwise known as the Middle East/North Africa Economic Summit, in Casablanca, Morocco, sponsored by the World Economic Forum and the Council on Foreign Relations. A number of us attending the conference went to a breakfast with Shimon Peres, who had been Israel's prime minister in the 1980s and would become prime minister again the following year, but who at the time was foreign minister. Peres had just engineered the Oslo Accords between his boss, Yitzhak Rabin, Israel's prime minister, and Yasser Arafat of the Palestine

Liberation Organization (the first direct agreement between Israel and the PLO), which had started as a secret dialogue between the two men. The mood in the region was optimistic about the opportunities for peace and for economic development and business expansion opportunities. So at the breakfast in Casablanca, I mentioned to Peres that I was interested in bringing Citibank to Israel.

I had made my first trip to Israel in the spring of 1992, as part of the Group of Thirty, which is an organization made up of academics, central bankers, finance ministers, and fellow financiers who analyze economic trends and global financial markets and institutions. We had traveled around the country, hosted by the governor of the Bank of Israel, Jacob Frenkel, whose efforts to hold the meeting I had supported. I got a feel for the business opportunities that could be available to Citibank there if only we had a branch.

It wasn't until the breakfast with Peres in Morocco two years later that I had a chance to mention my interest in opening in Israel.

"It's better a bank than a tank," responded Peres, who was given to making quips.

We agreed I would talk with Chairman Arafat as well, which I did. I told Arafat that we were contemplating more opportunities in the area and increasing our presence in the Middle East. He suggested that we extend our operations in Amman to include a branch in the West Bank. I committed only to pledging to become more involved in the economic development of the region, including the reopening of our branch in Lebanon, which was closed during the civil war in 1987. I encouraged him to keep up the PLO's rapport with Israel. I made it clear that opening in Israel was undoubtedly a possibility. I also told him that he should mobilize the Palestinian diaspora communities around the world to raise funds for Palestine—as Israel had done with the Jewish Diaspora—and not be so dependent on official handouts.

Another positive result of the Casablanca Summit was a side discussion that I had with some Egyptian business leaders, including Shafik Gabr, the respected Egyptian businessman who runs the multibillion-dollar conglomerate ARTOC Group and who was a founding member of the American Chamber of Commerce in Cairo in 1982. The idea was that if U.S. and Egyptian business leaders could get together to push an agenda of free trade, economic development, and reform of Egypt's then closed economy, it would help to foster a spirit of peace and development in the entire region. Ultimately, the result was the creation of the U.S.-Egypt Presidents' Council, a private-sector group with 10 representatives each from major U.S. and Egyptian corporations, including myself as a founding member. The U.S. side was headed by Vice President Al Gore, and the Egyptian side by President Hosni Mubarak. During my trip to Morocco, I was asked by a reporter from *Ha'aretz*, Israel's oldest daily newspaper, which is read by the country's elite, whether Citibank would consider opening a branch in the country.

"Why not open in Israel?" the *Ha'aretz* reporter had asked.

I told her I was thinking about it. The news made the paper in Israel and was picked up by major wire services.

Back in New York headquarters upon my return, some of my colleagues expressed uneasiness about the idea. Their particular concern was that such a move could possibly jeopardize relationships in some Arab countries. No Arab states except for Egypt and Jordan had diplomatic relations with Israel. The Arab League boycott—called in

1948 to isolate Israel economically and prevent Arab countries from doing business with the country—remained in full force. (Today only Lebanon and Syria adhere strictly to it.) But I pressed ahead.

A year later, we had made significant progress and had obtained the necessary board and regulatory approvals to open our first representative office in Tel Aviv. I was to attend the Gulf Economic Forum (GEF) in Bahrain in April 1995. The GEF was a regional forum that worked to promote business and investment interests in the Middle East, and was operated as a joint venture between the government of Bahrain and Dow Jones Telerate. The title of the conference was "New Agenda for Finance in the Middle East." When I told our people in the Middle East that I planned to make the announcement there, they were concerned for the same reasons that my colleagues in New York were. Yet I thought it was time to bring Israel into the broader business community—to get Arabs and Israelis working together on an economic basis in the region. Especially since we were about to reopen our operations in Beirut, which had been closed since the mid-1980s during Lebanon's long-fought war, I thought the timing was opportune. I had long been a big proponent of the idea that if you can open up trade, a political opening will follow. Trade, economics, and politics are inextricably linked. I wanted to make the announcement at the forum precisely because I felt that it was an example of the need to lead the way to more economic interchange in that area of the world. And this was a rare window of opportunity created by the nascent peace process, highlighted by the Rabin-Arafat accord in Oslo, to push ahead with business growth in the region. (Unfortunately, the optimism was to dim in November of that year, when Yitzhak Rabin was assassinated because of his signing of the Oslo Accords.) Forget the worries of my colleagues—it was the right thing to do, both for Citibank and the peoples of the region.

So, in the midst of that April speech, with roughly 400 experts on the Arab world in the audience, I was discussing the need for more opportunities to develop Gulf economies and attract Gulf capital, and I mentioned that Citi had plans to reopen its branch in Beirut. I also announced plans to open a representative office in Israel, in line with the spirit of the Casablanca Summit.

That was the spirit of rapprochement at the meeting where I had first mentioned my interest to Shimon Peres. I went on to talk about public share issues in Gulf countries being oversubscribed, which confirmed investor readiness in the area. That was the first time I had ever formally announced the opening of the Israeli office.

And then? Nothing happened. The head of the central bank of Iran was in the audience. So was Kurt Waldheim, the former U.N. secretary general and president of Austria, who was accused of complicity in war crimes while a German officer during World War II and who was barred from entering the United States. In the end there was no negative reaction at all.

A number of Arab bankers I spoke with at the forum told me that I was taking a realistic and bold view of the need to increase economic ties, which would ultimately help with the peace process in the region. So far we unfortunately see that the goal of peace has proven to be an elusive one, but there is no doubt that the idea of a peaceful resolution to the Arab-Israeli question has to be one of the most important diplomatic imperatives of our era.

Our representative office in Israel opened on Monday, February 5, 1996. When cutting the ribbon, I reemphasized what I had said a year earlier at the Gulf Economic Forum, calling the opening "a recognition of both the improvement in the macroeconomic conditions and the growing regional stability and business opportunities unfolding from the peace process."

We were the first major international banking institution to open a representative office in Israel, and among our first tasks were financing development and energy supply projects in the energy sector, underwriting Israel's privatization program, and facilitating trade between Israel and its neighbors. Jacob Frenkel declared the opening a "major event" and said that it would "help Israel in its strategy to incorporate into economies and capital markets worldwide." William McDonough, the president of the Federal Reserve Bank of New York, who was also in Israel, attended.

Three years later, we obtained permission to open a full-service branch in Tel Aviv. We were followed by HSBC and France's BNP, but today we remain the biggest and most profitable foreign bank operating in Israel—a clear demonstration of the fact that banks, as Peres had said, are indeed better than tanks, and that acting in accordance with your convictions is the surest way to achieve a goal.

CHINA: GUANGDONG DEVELOPMENT BANK

Another example of taking charge and making a decision despite counsel to the contrary came on the other side of the world: in this case, in long-drawn-out negotiations to acquire a share of a bank in China—a country where, in contrast to Israel, we had first set up operations more than 100 years ago. Not only did it work out in the short term, but the long-term outcome is likely to be better than anyone could have anticipated at the time.

In August of 2005, at the Aspen Meadows conference center in the midst of the Colorado Rocky Mountains, I had a discussion with Liu Mingkang, China's chief banking regulator, who was highly respected in the international banking community. We had arranged to meet for a chat after the opening dinner of the Program on the World Economy, which brings senior public- and private-sector leaders together every summer to discuss the solutions to major international economic problems.

We sat in the bar upstairs, and as I'd already had a couple of glasses of wine at dinner, I ordered a mineral water. Liu and I had served on the board of the Institute of International Finance (IIF) together, so I knew him to be very intelligent and knowledgeable about commercial banking. The IIF is a global association of financial institutions, including the world's largest commercial and investment banks.

I told Liu that Citigroup was interested in playing a role in the restructuring process for Guangdong Development Bank (GDB) that the government had initiated earlier in the year in return for an ownership stake and management rights. GDB had more than 500 branches in China. The province of Guangdong was situated just across the border from Hong Kong and was the home of China's manufacturing center; its capital, Guangzhou, was formerly known as Canton. Guangdong Development Bank was the largest bank in the wealthiest province in China.

At the time, GDB had assets of $47.9 billion, 12 million consumer customers, 9 million bank cardholders, 16,000 small and medium-sized business customers, and 12,474 employees. Its problems seemed to lie in its weak capitalization and its history of bad loans and risk taking.

China's second-largest insurance company, Ping An, was reported to be well along in the process of making an offer, but no final decision had been made. Liu responded that the deal apparently wasn't completed, and the government wanted to make the process as competitive as possible. Additionally, I raised the question of whether China would consider relaxing its law that prohibited foreigners from owning more than 20 percent of banks in China. Liu responded that any such decision to allow management control—meaning 51 percent or more—would have to be approved by the State Council, China's cabinet.

We'd already taken a small stake of 5 percent in Shanghai Pudong Development Bank in 2003, which was later diluted to 3.779 percent. I thought a stake in Guangdong Development Bank could be complementary.

For various reasons, two opportunities had already slipped through Citigroup's fingers. We had been presented with an opportunity to purchase a stake in China Bank of Communications two years earlier. I had considered it an opportunity to grab a foothold in the vast potential of China's banking system, but it didn't happen. China Bank of Communications was the second-oldest bank in China, and the leading bank in Shanghai before World War II. Its long history was important to its future success. So China Bank of Communications linked up with HSBC instead and did the deal.

Then Citigroup discussed buying a stake in China Construction Bank, but Bank of America got it.

So I looked at this potential stake in Guangdong Development Bank as our last, best opportunity. What made it especially interesting was that we thought it possible that we could purchase a stake big enough to confer management control, which would not have been the case with the other banks. With analysts of China's banking system concerned about nonperforming loans, both to state-owned enterprises and to individuals, gaining a management stake was an important way to ensure that we could clean up the loan portfolio and produce a responsible allocation of risk in the future. According to an audit report cited in *Caijing* magazine, China's leading business weekly, Guangdong Development Bank had net losses of more than 35 billion yuan, or about $4.23 billion. Its nonperforming loans amounted to 56 billion yuan, or $6.77 billion, which was 27 percent of its loan balance of 209 billion yuan ($25.27 billion)—an unusually high level—by the end of 2005. It also would be a way to ensure that we had the opportunity to influence the bank's strategic direction.

So at the Aspen meeting, I discussed the issue of control with Liu. I said that I would be especially interested in the deal if we could have it, and I promised to follow up with my colleagues. According to an account later published in *Caijing*, the government had originally approached Ping An the year before and asked for 10 billion yuan ($1.2 billion) to transfer full ownership of the bank, thinking that it would settle for 7 to 8 billion yuan. At the time, Ping An had offered just 3 billion yuan ($363 million), setting off China's wooing of foreign investors.

That night, when I returned to my room, I called our country head in China, Rich Stanley. It was morning in

Shanghai, and he was at his desk. I recounted my conversation with Liu. He said he thought it was a good idea, but he was skeptical. What about Ping An? Didn't they have it all tied up? I told him that there might be an opportunity for an outside partner and the potential for management control as well.

The next day, with New York two hours ahead of Aspen, I awoke early and phoned our then CEO, Chuck Prince.

"We've missed out on Communications. We missed out on China Construction. Our desire to increase our stake in Shanghai Pudong has not yet been approved by the regulators. So I think this is a unique opportunity to move ahead," I told Prince.

He was listening intently. "Sounds interesting," he responded. But, Prince asked, could we get management control?

Next, we got the steps underway: letters and expressions of interest, and the signing of a confidentiality agreement. Then we did our due diligence. The Guangdong government had at first picked 12 organizations out of 40 that were expressing interest in acquiring a stake, including 6 foreign institutions and 6 local. Of those, just 6 were chosen to conduct due diligence and make a preliminary offer; then 4 were chosen to conduct full due diligence and make formal bids.

The information memo that we all received from the government as part of this process of presenting an offer said that foreign investors could take management control after the restructuring was completed. At the same time, Guangdong government officials reiterated verbally the possibility that China might revise the 20 percent limit on foreign capital investments. When China's investment bankers asked us how much we might pay for an 85 percent stake, either by ourselves or as part of a consortium, that was really cause for excitement. We started pulling together a group of interested investors and bid 24.1 billion yuan, or $2.9 billion. But later came word that perhaps foreign control could amount to only 51 percent.

Ping An's new offer was 22 billion yuan ($2.66 billion), sweetened with a cash offer to the Guangdong government, according to *Caijing* magazine. France's Société Générale had partnered with Sinopec, the Chinese oil and gas giant, to bid 23.5 billion yuan ($2.84 billion). DBS (Development Bank of Singapore) made a lower offer that dropped it from serious contention. That left us, plus the two other contenders.

In December, I decided to go to Guangzhou, the gritty industrial capital of Guangdong province, and meet with senior members of the province's government. I drove up for the day from Hong Kong, where I was attending a client conference. Rich Stanley had flown down from our office in Shanghai. I reached Liu from the car phone as I was crossing the border into China. He told me that although there were rumors that foreign investors would be allowed to take a 40 percent stake, the existing rules mandated that combined ownership by foreign banks could not exceed 25 percent, with no more than 20 percent being held by a single foreign institution. I told him that I was disappointed, but that Citi was still interested in continuing our talks.

In Guangzhou, we met for tea in a formal hall of the Guangdong government offices, a room with chairs down both sides. I told the provincial representatives that I had come representing our senior management in New York, and that it was very important to us at Citigroup to be able to work with the government to turn this bank around.

I explained that Citibank had a long history in China, as well as a long commitment to the country under our predecessor, the International Banking Corp., the first U.S. bank in China, in 1902. I told them that the Citibank flag from China now takes pride of place, suspended from a wooden dowel, on the central wall of our second-floor boardroom at headquarters in New York. It is the first thing you see when you walk in.

We were nicknamed *Hua Qi*, or "Flower Flag" Bank, in those days because the Chinese referred to the U.S. flag as the "flower flag" and we were an American bank. Our flag, which resembled the U.S. flag, had flown outside our branch on Shanghai's Bund from the 1920s to the 1940s before we were forced to give up our branches to the Japanese during the occupation in World War II. We briefly reopened in 1945 before exiting in 1949, when Mao Zedong's Communist forces took over. We were also the first U.S. bank to reopen in China, after being allowed back into the country in 1983. We are still called *Hua Qi* Bank in Chinese to this day.

After a few cups of tea and a few long speeches, dutifully translated by official interpreters, the officials said that they were impressed by Citibank's long history in China and its dedication to the country, and that they and the Guangdong government would take that into account when the final decision was reached. In the meantime, however, a number of details still needed to be worked out.

But then the Chinese side went silent for months. Apparently what was holding up the deal was the okay from

Guangdong government officials. I made a second trip to see the provincial government, reiterating our interest in the deal and in helping to develop China.

There was, in fact, a strategy behind the Chinese indecision. By dangling the issue of management control while the bidding continued, the Chinese successfully captured the attention of foreign investors and boosted the prices that we would be willing to pay.

Then, in April 2006, Guangdong Province received formal notice from the China Banking Regulatory Commission (CBRC) in Beijing—the agency headed by Liu—confirming that combined ownership by foreign banks could not exceed 25 percent, with no more than 20 percent being held by a single foreign institution.

For several months, we worked with the People's Bank of China, the regulators, and the government. After all these meetings, we had to decide whether to proceed. I still thought, as did our local management, that the deal, even with restrictions, would be in the best interests of Citi, and of China as well. As we sought to find some other way of structuring the deal that would replicate some of the benefits of management control, I worked hard to sell it to my colleagues and the board back in New York.

I convinced them to move ahead.

Our signing ceremony was scheduled for 4 p.m. on November 16, 2006, at the Guangdong Development Bank executive offices in downtown Guangzhou. It was a windowless room with a long, formal table, mauve chairs, and green carpeting. Our consortium was to buy nearly 86 percent of Guangdong Development Bank for the bid price we had first put on the table. We would take a 20 percent stake, as would the local companies China Life Insurance

Company and State Grid (an electric power transmission company). CITIC Trust (a unit of the state-owned investment group formerly known as China International Trust and Investment) would take 12.85 percent, Pu Hua Investment (which was later dropped from the consortium) would take 8 percent, and IBM Credit would take 4.74 percent. The combined total taken by foreigners—our bank, plus IBM Credit—would be less than 25 percent. While we had originally set out to gain management control, we negotiated a pivotal agreement: we would have our stake frozen for six years, and the rest of the shareholders for three years. If any of them wanted out of the deal, Citigroup would have the first option to purchase their shares, subject to a change in the foreign ownership cap.

The local government had invited the broadcasting giant CCTV, as well as dozens of reporters from news outlets around the world, to witness the signing for the television news. Dow Jones, Bloomberg, Reuters—all were there, along with Chinese reporters from every major publication in China. But as 4 p.m. passed and the room began to buzz with anticipation, there was a problem. Despite assurances that all outstanding issues would be resolved by the time of the signing, at the last minute, one of our Chinese shareholders felt that it could not sign the deal. Our Citi team was running between the conference room, several holding rooms off to the side, and the canteen, where our lawyers had set up camp.

The signing ceremony was pushed back to 7 p.m. as lawyers for all sides, as well as our team, rushed from room to room trying to work out the final provisions that would reassure our Chinese partner.

As the hour of 8 p.m. neared, I knew that I had to take action. We could delay no longer. We had to go ahead with the signing ceremony without all agreements in place. Too much was at stake, and a failure to sign would have been an embarrassment for all of us, including our Chinese partners and the Guangdong provincial government. If we didn't proceed, some of our other shareholders might have wanted to back out. We would have been blamed for letting the deal fail, and that failure might jeopardize our future goals in China. We had built up tremendous expectations in the press and in the government.

Also, Hank Paulson, the U.S. secretary of the Treasury at the time, was to lead a high-level delegation to China a few weeks later to discuss trade and economic relations. The delegation was to include Federal Reserve Chairman Ben Bernanke, U.S. Trade Representative Susan Schwab, Commerce Secretary Carlos Gutierrez, and Labor Secretary Elaine Chao. They planned to meet with President Hu Jintao, Premier Wen Jiabao, and Vice Premier Wu Yi, China's trade czar. News of the deal was to be announced as progress in U.S.-China economic and trade relations. Tensions were high over China's refusal to allow its currency to float freely, as well as its enormous trade surplus with the United States, so U.S. officials wanted to have some positive developments to discuss.

Our image, built on nearly 100 years since we first went to China, was at stake. Damn the torpedoes, full speed ahead.

"Do it," I instructed. "I'll take responsibility with Chuck and the board."

I walked into the room with Rich Stanley and Bob Morse, our head of corporate and investment banking in

Asia-Pacific, and I took a seat in the front row. Li Handong, the deputy director of the Guangdong Financial Affairs Office, began delivering his speech about the historic nature of this deal and commemorating the great day for China and for the world. I gave a speech as well. But our team was still running in and out of the conference room, notebooks and documents in hand, and into the canteen next door, all in the name of trying to secure the final signature of our holdout partner. Finally, we could delay no longer, and my colleagues and the remainder of our consortium partners took their seats and signed, to the flash of photographic bulbs and the blinding lights of the television cameras.

Our lawyers pulled me out of the front row and told me that going ahead was the worst thing I could have done. We would lose our leverage over the holdout partner, and the deal might fall apart.

But it didn't. The shareholder came around four days later and finally signed the deal.

In the car on the long drive back to Hong Kong that night, and in my room at the Ritz-Carlton in Hong Kong when I returned at 2:30 in the morning, I had no second thoughts. I had done the right thing, both for Citibank and for China.

The confirmation of how right that decision was came not only with the Chinese partner's signing a few days later, but also on the balance sheets of Guangdong Development Bank. Within three years of closing the transaction, nonperforming loans had fallen from 5.8 percent to 2.3 percent of the portfolio. The bank's net asset value rose from $1.68 billion as of the end of 2006 to more than $3 billion at the end of 2008—an increase of more than 80 percent.

Operating revenue more than doubled in the same time period. The plan was also to prepare a public share offering by 2011, pending regulatory approval. Shareholder approval, including from Citigroup, was granted in early 2010. The evidence of decisive decision making is right there on the bottom line.

————

THESE THREE EXAMPLES show that in cases where you are faced with challenges to your leadership, timorous advice from cautious colleagues or legal counsel, or last-minute snafus that threaten to derail your progress, it pays to keep your wits about you. You should have the courage of your convictions, stick by your decisions, and push ahead. Be proactive and courageous, and you will be rewarded in the end—maybe not with a box of Cuban cigars from Fidel Castro, but with the mark of leadership.

BIBLIOGRAPHY

NICARAGUA

Cruz, Arturo, Jr. *Memoirs of a Counter-Revolutionary.* New York: Doubleday, 1989.

Khatami, Jim. "Consultants to the Third World." *Multinational Monitor* 2, no. 11, March 1981.

Roberts, Charles. "Nicaragua: The Unfolding Scene." *Multinational Monitor* 2, no. 2, March 1980.

"Selected Biographies of Resistance Leaders." Document 4, Documents on the Nicaraguan Resistance, U.S. Department of State, Bureau of Public Affairs, Office of Public Communication, Editorial Division. http://en.wikisource.org/wiki/

————

Documents_on_the_Nicaraguan_Resistance/Document_4, accessed May 19, 2009.

"Southern Front Contras: The Contra Story." General Reports-Cocaine, Central Intelligence Agency. https://www.cia.gov/library/reports/general-reports-1/cocaine/contra-story/south.html, accessed May 19, 2009.

"Whither Managua? Evolution of a City's Morphology." International Society of Civil and Regional Planners, 42nd ISoCaRP Congress, Istanbul, September 2006.

THE MIDDLE EAST AND ISRAEL

"Citibank Opens Representative Office Here." *Jerusalem Post*, February 6, 1996, p. 8.

CHINA

"Citigroup's Guangdong Dev Bank Plans Listing by 2010." Reuters, June 27, 2007.

"GDB Gets Shareholders' Nod to Raise 15b Yuan." *China Daily*, April 9, 2010. http://www.chinadaily.com.cn/bizchina/2010-04/09/content_9709217.htm.

Solomon, Deborah. "Paulsen Tempers Expectations for China Visit." *Wall Street Journal*, December 7, 2006, p. A6.

Yu Ning and Ji Minhua. "The Hot Battle for GDB." *Caijing*, pp. 32–45.

ANTICIPATE PROBLEMS BY VISUALIZING IMPACT

*How "Windows on Risk" Shielded
Citibank from the Asian Crisis,
a Phone Call Helped Save Uruguay,
and Rupert Murdoch Came to Like Bankers*

Having the foresight to think ahead can prevent a small situation from turning into a crisis. Many times in my career, I have been faced with situations that I realized could turn into serious problems if they were not addressed properly—if I did not take action and convince others to do the same. This was not always easy, and it required persistence and stamina along the way. The following three stories demonstrate the importance of seeing trouble ahead and taking measures to avert it.

In the 1990s, Citibank's then CEO, John Reed, had the idea for a new risk-assessment system called "Windows on Risk," which I implemented and headed. It was that system that forecast the Asian financial crisis of 1997–1998, allowing Citibank to take steps to minimize its exposure to the region. In Uruguay in 2002, the country was feeling the impact of the crisis in Argentina and was facing a liquidity problem. My phone call to the head of the International Monetary Fund (IMF) helped to free up an IMF emergency loan that kept the economy from going under. The case of Rupert Murdoch's News Corp. in the early 1990s was similar. When Murdoch found himself overburdened with debt, my colleagues at Citibank worked to refinance $7.6 billion of that debt, but found the deal hard to sell. When I was called in to help, I quickly recognized that a failure to refinance such an enormous international company would have ripple effects around the world and affect the global economy. I made this point to my fellow bankers in multiple markets and got the deal we had negotiated with Murdoch sold to the rest of the banking community.

The examples given here demonstrate the need for crisis prevention—getting out in front of problems and anticipating them. You need the foresight to recognize when a small crisis might turn into a large one. The way to do that is to step back and see the big picture. Learn how to understand the motivations, strengths, and weaknesses of all the players, and then figure out how to maneuver accordingly to keep small crises from turning into big ones.

WINDOWS ON RISK

In June 1992, our CEO, John Reed, walked into a colleague's office with a drawing. It was a piece of grid paper, and he had drawn six square boxes on it. Above them were the following words: Credit, Market, Risk Rating, Geography, Product, and Industry.

The boxes looked like windows, small frameworks through which we could view what could go wrong in the world. We ended up calling what came out of that idea "Windows on Risk."

Reed asked me, as senior risk officer, to head the development of Windows on Risk. On a Sunday morning, November 15, 1992, Reed called a meeting. It was a cold autumn day, and we met in a conference room at the Hyatt Hotel in Greenwich, Connecticut, near where Reed was then living. After considerable work by one of our vice presidents, David Martin, on how to develop the windows Reed had drawn on the grid paper into a project, we now had a plan to implement. Previously, Reed said, we did not understand the risks in the financial environment or the work that Citibank was undertaking within it. He turned to me and asked me to take charge.

One of our biggest achievements was predicting the Asian financial crisis of 1997 and reducing the bank's exposure in Asia before the worst of the crisis hit. Later, we also anticipated problems such as those in Japan and Russia, and those in the technology realm—and took actions to protect Citibank's bottom line.

In the early 1990s, the world was experiencing a financial crisis. A recession had begun in the third quarter of 1990, following the outbreak of the first Gulf War and the subsequent rise in oil prices. Then, troubles in the commercial real estate sector and in leveraged buyouts (LBOs), coupled with losses in our Latin America portfolio, led Citicorp to lose $5.8 billion in market value in 1990, and then in 1991 register a net loss of $457 million and suspend dividends for the first time in the bank's history. Consumer loan write-offs in this period rose by nearly $1 billion.

The idea, going forward, was not to be caught off guard again—to perceive the risks and be prepared to take action before any damage resulted. It wasn't just about credit and market risk; rather it was a comprehensive view of all types of risk: operational, technological, legal, and so on, and the linkages among them.

Banks are mirrors of their risk environment. The trick is being able to see the image clearly. What was clear, based on the problems that Citibank was facing at the time, was that the command-and-control structures that Citibank had previously been using didn't work.

Embedding risk management into every sector of the enterprise—breaking down the silos that had allowed operations to run their own risky ventures without considering the risks to the whole corporation—was the only way to implement a totally complete view.

This was the first time that Citibank began to look at risk across the company in a comprehensive way, rather than seeing it as affecting a bunch of separate enterprises that happened to be housed in the same institution.

Windows on Risk, then, began to monitor the state of the economy in various countries and the extent to which the bank's exposure to lending, underwriting, or trading could be affected. We used key risk factors, starting with about a dozen but ending up with 14 by the time the project wound down:

1. Client creditworthiness

2. Industry risks

3. Product risks

4. Obligor (debtor) concentrations

5. Global real estate risks

6. Country risks

7. Counterparty trading risks

8. Price, interest-rate, exchange-rate, and commodity risks

9. Liquidity risks

10. Equity and debt risks

11. Distribution and underwriting risks

12. Legal risks

13. Audit risks

14. Technology risks

What was innovative in Windows on Risk was the use of scenarios to evaluate multiple risks simultaneously and then to mandate specific courses of action as a result. We used "what if" scenarios, taking the idea from the White House situation room, and developed "trip wires." If we saw any of those trip wires (a natural disaster, a coup d'état, the resignation of a key minister, and so on), then we would stop and reassess the bank's business in that area.

We assigned each trip wire a percentage probability, such as 25 percent for widespread economic impact from a flu outbreak, and calculated the risk in the countries affected accordingly. The process was ever-changing according to ongoing developments. As the project evolved, we increasingly focused on the consumer and emerging-market sides of our business.

We invited out-of-the-box thinkers who were experts in their fields to warn us of new risks. Then we took action based on what they said and what the data were telling us.

We stress-tested our portfolios. At each meeting, a list of actions to mitigate risk was discussed, and people were held accountable for how they managed those risks.

Normal price fluctuations were closely scrutinized, and risks were monitored continually. For example, if the price of oil suddenly went up or down, we would look at the consequences for lending, both short term and medium term.

We instituted quarterly Windows on Risk review meetings in New York. The core participants included Reed; our vice chairman, Paul Collins; Pei-yuan Chia, head of consumer banking; and Onno Ruding, head of corporate banking for industrialized countries. We also invited the heads of our tech, audit, and legal departments, as well as various others. We held regional Windows meetings worldwide at least twice a year that focused on the specific issues within that region and other global issues.

At those meetings, we evaluated all the risk factors of the previous four months and made any necessary changes in Citibank's overall portfolio. Nothing replaces good individual credit judgment, but Windows on Risk helped us manage proper credit balance at a higher level.

No other institution used such a comprehensive risk-analysis mechanism. When we met with regulators in those difficult days of 1992, they were so impressed with the tool we had devised that they recommended that other banks come up with similar risk-management tools.

We believed that ours may have been the first enterprisewide risk-management system in the world.

In May 1996, we invited the noted economist Paul Krugman, who later became a columnist for the *New York Times* and won a Nobel Prize in economics, to come speak to our group.

It was more than a year before the Asian crisis began. In late 1994, Krugman had written an article called "The Myth of Asia's Miracle" for the influential policy journal *Foreign Affairs*. "There is nothing miraculous about the successes of Asia's 'tigers,'" he wrote. "Their rise was fueled by mobilizing resources—increasing inputs of machinery, infrastructure, and education—just like that of the now-derided Soviet economy." He argued that their growth was based solely on the race to manufacture exports, and that without a corresponding increase in domestic consumption, it could not be maintained by feeding U.S. and European imports. In other words, Asian growth was running out of steam. "The growth rates of the newly industrialized countries of East Asia will also slow down," he wrote.

Krugman was right, even if he was early. In fact, a greater crisis was on the horizon, caused by overborrowing and the resulting bubble fueling this mobilization of resources. It would take precisely two and a half more years.

In introducing Krugman to the Windows on Risk meeting, I mentioned Mexico's economic crisis of 1994, the Tequila Crisis. I said that Asia looked to be setting itself up for just as bad a situation, if not worse.

Krugman then spoke and backed up my thinking on Asia. In particular, he cited large current-account deficits and slowing growth, which would lead to a "potentially serious dislocation" in Southeast Asian economies. "The Southeast Asian numbers looked to me a lot like Mexico before the crisis," Krugman later recalled in an article. "I didn't buy the argument that Asian countries were so structurally superior to Latin American countries as to be immune."

Some Asia-is-immune thinkers argued that the region would be saved from crisis by its high savings rates and so-called Asian values, a poorly defined idea of difference that was later discredited in academia.

But in reality, Asia had an asset bubble that no amount of glossing over could evade. Financial bloodbaths always run red no matter where in the world they occur.

In Thailand, the baht had been pegged at a rate of 25 to the dollar for 10 years and was thought to be considerably overvalued; the country had high current-account deficits, a weak and poorly supervised financial system, and overlending in the real estate sector. And in South Korea, the top 10 *chaebol*, or business conglomerates, had debt-to-equity ratios averaging over 500 percent.

Real estate and financial institutions were the areas that were most at risk, not only in Thailand and South Korea, but in Indonesia and Malaysia as well. Citibank's retail and lending exposure in the region was considerable. We had 6.2 million accounts at 93 branches in 13 Asian markets (excluding India and Pakistan).

At the meeting, we compared Asia's exports to Latin America's after the Tequila Crisis, and we saw that the Asians would take longer to export their way out of a crisis. It was clear that we had to reduce risk, decrease lending, and protect Citibank portfolios from an oncoming crisis. We then scheduled a further review of Southeast Asia for our next Windows meeting, to be held July 24.

Subsequently, we gave the word to our business heads in Asia that they had to reduce risk. It wasn't very popular with them at first. Asia was in the midst of a boom. Throttling down the engine in the middle of a race seemed nuts from the perspective of those on the ground. But in New York, we knew that a crash was coming.

On a series of trips to the region that year, I had witnessed the Asian building boom and bubble for myself. It was clear that economies such as Thailand, Indonesia, and South Korea were overheating.

As a result, we changed our risk parameters, weeded out weak customers, and cut our exposure to troubled business sectors. We substantially reduced our exposure in Thailand and Indonesia.

I also sounded the alarm to the U.S. government. In September 1996, I had a conversation with U.S. Treasury Undersecretary for International Affairs Jeff Shafer, who later came to work for Salomon, which became part of Citigroup after the merger with Travelers in 1998. I met with him in his office in Washington, D.C., after I had just returned from yet another trip to Asia.

In Bangkok, I had met with Tarrin Nimmanahaeminda, Thailand's former finance minister, who had been replaced the previous year. He told me that the heavy buildup of foreign debt by Thai companies could lead to a crisis. He also said that "the steam was running out of the economy." When I checked Citibank's portfolios in our Bangkok office, I clearly saw the danger signs. Customers were falling behind on their loan payments.

Shafer listened to me with concern. He said he would look into it and find out what others were saying. After I left, he phoned the Finance Ministry in Thailand. Chatu Mongol Sonakul, then permanent secretary for finance and later the governor of the Bank of Thailand, was the great-grandson of a nineteenth-century Siamese king. He told Shafer that the Thai government wasn't concerned because what counted was the opinion of the Japanese banks,

Thailand's biggest creditors. He said that the Japanese had not expressed any concerns or cut bank lending—even though Citibank had.

So next Shafer phoned Japan and mentioned my concerns. He reached Eisuke Sakakibara, who at the time headed the Finance Ministry's international finance bureau. Sakakibara was known as "Mr. Yen" because of his policies that regularly moved the value of the Japanese currency against the dollar. He told Shafer that he would look into it and get back to him, but never did.

I began sounding the alarm in public as well. On March 17, 1997, I was attending the Inter-American Development Bank meeting in Barcelona and was quoted in an article in *Emerging Markets*, the newspaper of record for IMF, World Bank, and regional development bank meetings, as warning about excess liquidity in the system. "Capital flows are great coming in, but they can be disastrous washing out, and I just want to put that up as a marker to institutions," I said.

I was able to reach the broader public in a March 20 article in the *Financial Times*. "I've never seen such liquidity as I've seen today and I've been around a long time," I was quoted as saying. "We have to be careful in this environment that credit standards are maintained."

At a May 1997 meeting of the Asian Development Bank in Fukuoka, Japan, I still found few people who agreed with me. Officials in Thailand were already under attack by currency speculators who were trying to break the $1 = 25 baht peg, but Thai officials were confident that they could defend the baht. When I met Kang Kyung-shik, South Korea's finance minister, on the margins of the meeting, I mentioned my concerns. He blamed currency speculators rather than any endemic problems. He also said that an election was coming up in South Korea, and that the ruling party was not likely to make any policy changes before then. South Korean officials believed that they could still find all the funds they needed to meet their enormous debt obligations through the capital markets.

When the crisis finally hit in July 1997, Citibank was spared the worst of it. And then, during the crisis, we were able to expand our credit lines to qualified clients at the same time that others were cutting back. We became the beneficiaries of a flight to safety.

We also mobilized resources to manage through the tough credit environment. We were able to use the automated phone systems that we had instituted across Asia to notify any delinquent customers as soon as their credit card payments were 31 days past due. We also hired 300 outside debt collectors throughout the region and retrained hundreds of our employees, who previously had experienced only boom years, to handle the crisis.

Little did I know that I was going to be called in to help fix the problems, which I did later in South Korea (see Lesson 4).

In another Windows success story, we turned to technology risk as the subject of our guest speaker. I invited Tsutomu Shimomura, one of America's leading computer security experts. As the meeting got underway, he took out a brand-new cell phone, removed the back, fiddled around with it, and placed a call to a phone line in an office down the hall.

We listened in on speakerphone as he easily tapped into the person's voicemail with just a few presses of the dial pad. It was incredible to see how vulnerable we were to hackers. We immediately ordered that safeguards be put into place. Shimomura also warned us to tighten security at our call centers and for our satellite communications, which we did, thereby reducing our vulnerability to attack.

There were other successes of Windows in the six years that I ran it, small warnings all along the way that helped the bank manage risk and operate profitably and well.

Shortly after the 1998 merger with Travelers Group, I moved on from the job of senior risk officer. The Windows on Risk process, although highly successful, was soon phased out after my tenure and replaced with other risk-management tools that were then incorporated into Citigroup's risk-management process.

The lesson here is that first you need to have the vision to call problems early, and then you need to take action to head them off—sound warnings, reduce exposure, implement new systems, do whatever you need to do. This can save billions of dollars as well as reputations.

URUGUAY

By 2002, the ripple effects of Argentina's slide into defaulting on its $140 billion worth of foreign debt (see Lesson 6) were affecting an innocent neighbor, Uruguay. As a mini-financial center for the region, Uruguay had a solid reputation among investors for stable financial indicators and an investment-grade bond rating, one of just two in South America—until February 2002, that is.

Argentines and others in Latin America had long seen Uruguay as a banking safe haven and kept dollars in

Montevideo bank accounts. But during the Argentine crisis, with bank accounts in Buenos Aires frozen, Argentines began pulling out the only money they could access—in Uruguay. They made massive withdrawals, amounting to fully half of all deposits, prompting a run on the banks and leading to a plunge in the value of the Uruguayan peso. The run drained 80 percent of foreign reserves.

On top of that, Uruguay's economy depended on the country's being able to export half its production to Argentina and Brazil, where demand had dropped considerably. And in 2001, Uruguayan cattle suffered from an outbreak of foot-and-mouth disease, which halted exports of meat (20 percent of all exports) for the entire year. After averaging growth of 5 percent annually in the mid-1990s, Uruguay's economy shrank by 2 percent in 2001 and more than 10 percent in 2002. The unemployment rate rose to 20 percent, inflation surged, and the burden of paying off external debt doubled—to $10 billion, or the size of its entire economy. Uruguay needed an urgent bailout from the International Monetary Fund.

Yet a bailout was nowhere to be seen. Horst Köhler, the IMF's managing director, had been pummeled in the financial community for going too far and being too lenient with Argentina. The last thing he wanted to do was bail out Argentina's small neighbor as well.

In fact, the IMF position was that Uruguay should start a restructuring process that would require its bondholders to take a haircut as a precondition for the disbursement of previously pledged funds. The IMF reasoned that such a strategy would reduce Uruguay's total debt burden. And it would inflict pain on bondholders at a time when some senior IMF officials were trying to convince the private sector to support an international bankruptcy court for sovereign countries (see Lesson 5). But Uruguay wanted to restructure without asking its creditors to take a massive hit.

The IMF had pledged a total of $4.3 billion in standby credit for Uruguay, agreed to in increments since 2000 in exchange for the country's adherence to a structural reform program that included Uruguay's raising income taxes, which it had done. But the IMF continued to withhold the money.

By late July, the situation in Montevideo was worsening. The runs on the banks had become so acute that the government had no choice but to close them and declare a bank holiday. There were strikes, rock-throwing protests, and outbreaks of looting in supermarkets and shops. The violence came after the government ordered banks to close to try to stop people from withdrawing their savings.

That was when President Jorge Batlle called me in desperation. He was agitated on the phone, and he wanted me to call the IMF and the U.S. Treasury and intervene on Uruguay's behalf. On July 25, two of his senior officials (the head of the central bank and his minister of planning) had been in Washington seeking emergency IMF help, but they were turned away.

So Batlle was frantic when he called. I had met him on several occasions, and I could hear the desperation in his voice. He knew that I had a good working relationship with Köhler.

"They don't understand that Uruguay is a separate country from Argentina," he said. "We're a long-standing democracy. They're going to ruin us. You have to call the IMF."

I felt sorry for him, and for the plight of Uruguay. The country had been a trustworthy borrower. I had restructured Uruguay's debt twice before, in 1983 and then with the Brady bonds in 1991, and I had found that it had always lived up to its agreements.

Uruguay didn't want to be forced into a market-unfriendly course. Its crisis was simply one of liquidity, not of long-term economic mismanagement.

So I called Köhler. I told him that the contagion from Argentina was spreading. South America was a house of cards, and if Uruguay went under, then the contagion would keep spreading and affect many of the remaining economies as well. In addition, Brazil was increasingly becoming a concern. If the IMF did not act to stem this crisis and disburse the funds it had pledged, then it would spend the next decade bailing out the rest of the South American countries. I reminded him that Uruguay had a very good record of meeting its debt obligations.

An IMF loan, ultimately amounting to $2.8 billion, finally arrived in early August.

I wasn't the only one who helped. Batlle had phoned everyone he knew in New York and Washington to ask for support. He later credited the Federal Reserve Bank of New York for also arranging emergency financing before the IMF funds were disbursed.

In fact, President George W. Bush phoned Batlle directly in late July to tell him that U.S. emergency funding was on the way and that there would be a $1.5 billion bridge loan that would get the country through its crisis so that banks could reopen on August 5 after the bank holiday.

Up until that time, the Bush administration, which was fed up with Argentina and what it had viewed as the profligacy of the Clinton administration in bailing out Mexico, had pledged no more bailouts. Treasury Secretary Paul

O'Neill had said in an off-the-cuff remark on *Fox News* the previous week that in order for the United States to support future bailouts, it needed assurances that U.S. taxpayers' money wouldn't end up in the Swiss bank accounts of corrupt Latin American officials.

After the phone call of support from Bush, Köhler announced that he was releasing the previously pledged funds and increasing the standby credit by another $500 million.

That saved Uruguay from going under. It would have defaulted otherwise. The bank runs ceased, and bank deposits actually increased. Street violence stopped.

By the end of 2002, with the economy stabilizing, Uruguay was ready to go ahead with restructuring its debt. It was clear that the Uruguayans were serious about making the necessary adjustments.

Yet Finance Minister Alejandro Atchugarry and the head of the central bank, Isaac Alfie, had decided to choose Deutsche Bank and Merrill Lynch instead of Citibank to do the restructuring.

When I found out about it, I was on a plane to Brazil with Citibank's head of Latin American investment banking, Carlos Guimarães. He said that we had exhausted our approach and needed someone who was well known in Uruguay and was considered a friend of the country. He suggested that I reach Atchugarry by phone, which I did immediately from the air.

"This decision makes so little sense," I said into the receiver.

I reminded him of Citibank's and my own personal involvement in the previous restructuring in 1983 and in the Brady bonds. I told Atchugarry that restructuring isn't simple; it's open-heart surgery, and he needed a bank with an experienced team. I knew the country, had respect for the country, and could be more helpful to Uruguay than other financial institutions. I promised I would involve myself personally in the deal and get it done.

We had also just done a restructuring for Ecuador and were clearly the institution with the most experience in "reprofiling"—renegotiating the terms of a country's existing debt and helping the country reposition itself.

The Ecuador deal in 2000 had required bondholders to agree to a bond swap that replaced $6.46 billion worth of defaulted debt with new bonds carrying collective action clauses, which allowed a "supermajority" of bondholders to agree to terms that would apply to all. This eliminated the threat from vulture investors who wanted to extract more concessions by refusing to go along with the restructuring. Mexico had issued the first new bonds with collective action clauses (see Lesson 5), but Ecuador's swap was the first time that a country had replaced its old bonds with new ones that included the clauses.

We wanted to implement a similar plan for Uruguay. The country had $1.88 billion in debt amortization due in 2003 alone, and the IMF was making continued support for Uruguay conditional on a successful restructuring.

By the time I got back to New York, there was a fax from Montevideo waiting for me, asking for the involvement of just Citibank and Deutsche Bank. Merrill Lynch had dropped out.

So we submitted a proposal for the restructuring. A month later, Deutsche Bank decided not to go ahead and resigned from the deal. In the end, we were the guys who got it done, on our own.

In March we launched road shows in the United States, Europe, and Japan to discuss terms with creditors around the world and continued negotiations into April. Uruguay won the support of 94 percent of the bondholders for the deal.

In May 2003, the government agreed to restructure $5.3 billion—almost half of its $11 billion foreign debt—pushing the repayment dates back five years. That year, Uruguay registered 12 percent GDP growth.

The consultation with the bondholders and the market made a difference. It showed that the country wanted to make a transparent approach to its creditors. As a result, I received a congratulatory letter from Treasury Secretary John Snow praising the "positive development" of the inclusion of collective action clauses. "This is truly a historic development in the progress of sovereign debt and I trust will be widely and duly noted by both sovereign debt issuers and the private marketplace," Snow wrote.

By October, Uruguay had come back to the market voluntarily to issue a new, inflation-indexed bond—unheard-of speed for a comeback. Five years later, after following the IMF program, Uruguay improved its debt profile by repaying $1.1 billion to the IMF.

If I hadn't pushed, Uruguay might not have come out of the crisis as well as it did. Uruguay needed bankers with experience in dealing with something so complex. The IMF needed a push to get it to help keep Uruguay from going under and prevent the contagion in Latin America from spreading. That call to the IMF made a difference in its decision to disburse the Uruguay loan.

RUPERT MURDOCH

In late 1990, our CEO, John Reed, and one of our executive vice presidents, Alan MacDonald, asked me to have dinner with Rupert Murdoch. A team at Citibank led by Ann Lane, who headed corporate debt restructuring, had been trying to put together a debt refinancing deal, but it was having trouble selling the deal to the other banks involved. Murdoch's News Corporation, it seemed, was having trouble meeting its short-term debt obligations. It was becoming too big a risk in the marketplace, and the banks were worried about bankruptcy. They had serious concerns about Murdoch's capacity to run News Corp. because of the enormous amounts of debt he had taken on.

Murdoch's News Corp., an Australian multimedia conglomerate with earnings of $1.4 billion and falling, plus a balance sheet that was $1.7 billion in the red, owed its creditors $7.6 billion—an indebtedness on a par with that of an entire small country. The company was valued at $26 billion under Australian accounting rules, but that valuation was not all it appeared to be: half of it was made up of "intangibles," the theoretical valuations that News Corp. placed on such things as film rights, newspaper titles, and TV licenses.

Under stricter U.S. accounting standards, News Corp.'s value was more like $3.8 billion—exactly half of what it owed its creditors. The result was that Moody's Investors Service lowered News Corp.'s rating to B-1.

Citibank alone was owed $832 million, but the biggest lender was Commonwealth Bank of Australia, to the tune of $973 million. So many banks were involved that if even one bank held out, it could push Murdoch into bankruptcy. News Corp.'s international bonds were yielding 47 percent because of concern over a possible bankruptcy—the kind of returns one would normally expect from an overly indebted African or Latin American country that was at risk of default.

Murdoch had spent the 1980s turning his company from an international publishing giant into a multimedia conglomerate. In the run up to and during the decade, Murdoch purchased and/or sold—on top of his collection of British newspapers, the *Sun*, the *Times* of London, and the *Sunday Times*—Sky TV in Britain; Triangle Publishing, which owned *TV Guide* and at the time was the largest media purchase in history; the *South China Morning Post* in Hong Kong; and a number of tabloid and other newspapers in the United States, including the *Boston Herald*, the *Chicago Sun-Times*, and the *New York Post*.

He also owned Ziff Publishing, with consumer titles that included *Modern Bride, Popular Photography, Yachting*, and *Car & Driver*, 20 percent of Pearson PLC, which owns the *Financial Times*; Harper & Row publishing, which he merged with William Collins & Sons to create HarperCollins; part of the Warner Brothers movie studios, plus 50 percent of Twentieth Century Fox; and a number of newspapers that had formerly been owned by his father in their country of origin, Australia.

Murdoch had also launched a TV network, Fox—which at the time was losing $2 million a week.

But this was the 1980s. Overleveraging was *du jour*. People with high tolerance for risk were making great fortunes.

Yet Murdoch had never been known for his ability or desire to amass a fortune. He was once quoted as saying that he "didn't care about making money." Subsequently, he weathered years of losses at the *New York Post,* the *Times* of London, and the conservative magazine *The Weekly Standard.* And he later proved his motivation to be other than the bottom line by buying the *Wall Street Journal* in 2007, for which, many analysts said at the time, he overpaid at a price of $5.6 billion, once again taking on debt at the peak of the newspaper's value, just as the business model of the newspaper industry was starting to unravel.

Back in 1990, the situation was far worse. The company was losing value in the markets every day as word of Murdoch's debt problems became known. Murdoch tried to generate more cash flow by buying more and more assets and taking on more and more debt.

I knew we had to act. News Corp. was at the front end of a wave of corporate troubles. The first Gulf War had begun in August after Iraq had invaded Kuwait. The resulting spike in the price of oil was beginning to have an impact on the U.S. economy, causing inflation and a 1.5 percent contraction in GDP in the third quarter. A real estate bubble had burst. The downturn was to last through the first quarter of 1991.

Going into a recession made urgent action to save News Corp. all the more crucial. Given the troubles in the U.S. economy, a bankruptcy by News Corp. would have caused the kind of instability that the world's economy might not have been able to handle just then. The fall of such a major player with such a huge debt load would have created or exacerbated systemic risk.

But before I could vouch for Murdoch, I first had to meet with him. We arranged for Ann Lane and me to have dinner with him at La Côte Basque restaurant in New York.

He brought his then wife Anna, who appeared to be a source of strength for him.

I wanted to be sure that he was prepared to cooperate fully, to make the necessary sacrifices, and to work hard to complete the deal—to get on a plane himself to talk with other bankers and reassure them that he was going along with the restructuring that was proposed.

Over the course of nearly three hours of dinner discussion, I became convinced that he was. Murdoch seemed like a boxer in the last rounds of a fight. He conceded that he had taken on too much debt. He agreed that he hadn't really spent the time he should have on his financials, and that he hadn't seen the recession coming.

He recognized that he needed to strengthen the role that finance played in his business. He understood his situation and said that he was willing to take advice. He said that he knew he was in trouble, and that he would do what I asked of him. He gave me five telephone numbers where he could be reached at all times, night or day: New York, California, London, Hong Kong, and Australia.

I was impressed with how straightforward he was. Murdoch is known for being disconcertingly direct. He had checked out my background, he said, and had been told that I was the one who could help him.

"I've got to be honest with you," Murdoch said to me. "I don't much care for bankers. I never had much time for them."

"By the time we're through, you're damn well going to like them," I responded. And I was right.

January 31, 1991, was a crucial date. At that time, $2 billion in News Corp. debt would be due and could not be rolled over. If the obligations could not be met and refinancing could not be worked out, News Corp. would become insolvent within a few months.

When I got back to my office the following day, I started making calls to my fellow bankers. I had a network of U.S. regional banks—First Chicago, Mellon, and the like. My message was that News Corp. was so large that its collapse could have a very serious impact on the international economy. I told everyone I phoned that they must help. I put my whole international debt restructuring team on the case as well, working in conjunction with Ann Lane's domestic corporate restructuring group.

I also phoned Jacques de Larosière, who at the time was the head of the French central bank, the Banque de France. He understood the urgency of the issue. He was going to be chairing an upcoming meeting of central bank governors, who meet monthly in Basel, Switzerland, under the auspices of the Bank for International Settlements (BIS), an association of central bankers. While there, he conveyed to the central bank governors of Europe and the United States, plus Japan, that a failure to reach agreement on restructuring Murdoch's debt could be serious. He asked them for support in getting their countries' banks on board with the Murdoch package. Once those banks knew that the big players were on board, they would go along as well.

That worked for about 90 percent of the banks. But the final 10 percent of the banks were proving tough. They thought they could hold out for better terms.

So I worked the phones over Christmas of 1990, doing my utmost to persuade the holdout banks to participate in the deal. By early 1991, many banks had agreed to reschedule, particularly if they could be assured that others were going along. I also phoned Murdoch several times to insist that he get on the phone with bankers as well to make his case. It was rare for CEOs to talk directly to banks. They usually leave that task to their CFOs. But Murdoch got down in the trenches and did his part.

On February 1, 1991, we announced the agreement: $7.6 billion in loans would be extended for another three years.

To express his appreciation, Rupert and Anna Murdoch flew to Paris for the ceremony at the Banque de France later that year when I was awarded France's Légion d'honneur by Jacques de Larosière for my role in leading Latin American debt restructurings.

Speaking on the fiftieth anniversary of my tenure at Citigroup in September 2007, Murdoch said: "When the real crunch came, Bill came in and got us over the line. By dogged hard work, Bill forms important and great relationships. Everyone knows Bill. Everyone trusts Bill."

It turned out that Rupert Murdoch had come to like some bankers after all. It was his willingness to face reality, recognize his mistakes, and do what was necessary as CEO that demonstrated why and how he had built such a successful empire. And on my part, it was the foresight to envisage the implications that a News Corp. failure could have on the world and on the global economy of the time that made the difference in halting any negative repercussions.

———

WHAT YOU NEED to consider when taking action is the future impact. Ask yourself, if I don't take a course of action, where will this situation end up in three months' time? In six months' time? In a year's or two years' time? In all cases,

evaluate the risk, the impact, and the reward. Visualize it
and then act accordingly.

BIBLIOGRAPHY

WINDOWS ON RISK

Citicorp Annual Report, 1990, pp. 2–3.

Citicorp Annual Report, 1991, pp. 1–3.

Clifford, Mark L., and Pete Engardio. *Meltdown: Asia's Boom, Bust and Beyond.* Paramus, N.J.: Prentice Hall, 2000, pp. 216–217.

Kraus, James R. "Ready for the Next Recession." *American Banker,* November 8, 2004, p. 4.

Krugman, Paul. "The Myth of Asia's Miracle." *Foreign Affairs,* November/December 1994.

Martin, David. "Windows on Risk: Meeting Notes & Follow-Ups." May 16, 1996.

Martin, David, and Michael Power. "The End of Enterprise Risk Management." AEI-Brookings Joint Center for Regulatory Study, August 2007.

McDermott, Darren. "Citibank Uses Latin American Lessons in Asia." *Wall Street Journal,* December 29, 1997, p. A6.

Starr, Peter. *Citibank: A Century in Asia.* Singapore: Editions Didier Millet, 2002, p. 154.

URUGUAY

Barham, John. "Cooking Up a New Solution." *Latin Finance,* June 1, 2003, p. 10.

Bissio, Roberto. "Uruguay: IMF Loan Only a Palliative." Third World Network. http://www.twnside.org.sg/title/twr143c.htm, accessed May 22, 2009.

Goodman, Joshua, with Pete Engardio. "Uruguay: A Well-Executed Model for Debt Workouts." *BusinessWeek,* September 29, 2003.

Salmon, Felix. "Uruguay's Elegant Transformation." *Euromoney,* February 1, 2004.

"A Swap Staves Off Default." *Latin Finance,* February 1, 2004, p. 36.

"Uruguay Hit by Strikes and Violence." BBC News, August 2, 2002. http://news.bbc.co.uk/2/hi/business/2166706.stm, accessed August 4, 2009.

Rupert Murdoch

"Fifty Years of Service: William R. Rhodes." Citigroup Corporate Affairs, Disc 4, Business Leaders and Dignitaries, 2008.

Lemann, Nicholas. "Paper Tigers: What Media Moguls Make." *New Yorker,* April 13, 2009, pp. 72–77.

Light, Deborah, and John Lyons. "Murdoch Wins Time to Rewrite History." *The Age,* February 2, 1991, p. 1.

Shawcross, William. *Murdoch.* London: Chatto & Windus, 1992, pp. 515–519.

Wolff, Michael. *The Man Who Owns the News: Inside the Secret World of Rupert Murdoch.* New York: Random House, Doubleday, 2008, pp. 17, 175–186, 294.

EXECUTE IN A TIMELY FASHION

*Managing Citibank's 1991 Loan Crisis,
Creating "Critical Mass" during the
Latin American Debt Crisis, and
Implementing Argentina's Brady Bonds*

Time is your enemy. There is never enough of it. Therefore, there's nothing more important than an attitude of determined relentlessness when it comes to getting things done in a timely fashion. All too often, people are content to let situations move forward at a slow pace, figuring that in time things will take care of themselves. Yet such inaction, refusing to move steadfastly forward toward a timely solution, is a recipe for letting crisis situations fester dangerously. The best way to execute in a meaningful manner is to be persistent and to stick to your guns. In the following three examples, I show how being unrelenting in pursuit of a goal resulted in positive outcomes.

When Citibank faced a debt crisis in its lending portfolios in 1991, I had to prove to regulators that we were taking appropriate actions by writing down our debts rather than adding to our reserves, as was the practice of other banks at the time. We worked day and night to go over our loans one by one. The result was that we received a satisfactory audit report just as the markets feared that Citibank might topple under its bad debts. During the Latin American debt crisis that began in 1982, my team and I worked tirelessly to persuade fellow banks to cooperate with the International Monetary Fund, the World Bank, governments, and central banks to provide timely solutions to the indebtedness problems of Mexico, Argentina, Brazil, and other countries in the region. And in Argentina, when it came down to the wire in implementing a Brady bond solution to its well-needed debt restructuring, I insisted that our negotiating teams work all night to get the deal done.

These lessons illustrate that working on a problem without stopping, with relentlessness and persistence, is the best way to bring about a favorable solution. You must seize the time you have and make the most of it, and don't let up—even if it means sleepless nights—until you are finished.

COMPTROLLER OF THE CURRENCY

The situation in Hong Kong in early August 1991 was almost out of control. People with deposits at Citibank's branches there were reacting to a remark made by Rep. John Dingell, a Democrat from Michigan who chaired the House Committee on Energy and Commerce, at congressional hearings in Washington, D.C., aimed at prohibiting banks from expanding their business franchises. Citibank was "technically insolvent" and "struggling to survive," he said, spooking the markets and causing Citi's share price to plunge.

But even more spooked were the Citibank depositors in Hong Kong, who had read his comments in a local newspaper. People in Hong Kong had already been traumatized by the closing of the local branch of Bank of Credit and Commerce International (BCCI), which, since BCCI lacked depositor's insurance, had wiped out a number of savings accounts. They were understandably nervous about any rumors of another insolvent bank.

But Citibank was in no such condition, and Hong Kong was the only place in the world to experience a panic. Senior management at Citibank had refuted Dingell's assertion and assured the public that we had enough cash to go around. Our sound standing had been backed by the chairman of the Federal Deposit Insurance Corporation (FDIC). Americans shrugged off what Dingell had said. Still, depositors in Hong Kong lined up to take out their money. We had it, and we doled it out just as fast as we could get armored trucks to our various branches—but not before the bank run was picked up on television news cameras and broadcast around the world.

Dingell's remarks and those images from Hong Kong attracted the attention of regulators, whose pique was already heightened by a real estate crisis that was hitting banks all over the United States.

In 1990, the real estate market had plunged. In an all-too-familiar story, overbuilding and overlending were to blame. The Japanese, who had invested heavily in U.S. commercial real estate, including the famous purchase of Rockefeller Center, were facing the bursting of their own bubble back home. They beat a retreat from real estate, exacerbating the drop.

The federal banking regulators, led by Jimmy Barton, deputy comptroller from the Office of the Comptroller of the Currency, an independent bureau of the U.S. Treasury, took over four banks in Texas. Then, in January 1991, the Bank of New England warned that bad loans would cause it to report a loss of $450 million in the fourth quarter of 1990. Depositors made a run on its branches and withdrew $1 billion. Regulators intervened, essentially shut it down, and then began scrutiny of the rest of the country's financial institutions, causing a credit freeze.

The markets feared that Citibank might be next.

Shortly after Dingell's remarks and the run in Hong Kong, our CEO, John Reed, told a meeting of business executives in Chicago that Citibank was engaged in major real estate loan write-offs that would continue far longer than expected. Property values could be expected to fall another 30 percent before they stabilized, he said. When his remarks were reported in the *Wall Street Journal*, they caused a further decline in the company's stock price. In the third quarter of 1991, Citicorp posted a loss of $885 million and eliminated its dividend for the first time since 1813.

By fall, Barton and his team of banking examiners had taken over several offices at Citibank headquarters at 399 Park Avenue. They were combing through every aspect of our books in an effort to determine whether the government should intervene in our operations and replace our management, too.

Known as a man who really shook things up, Barton was every bit the stern bank examiner, a real-life version of the Mr. Carter who came to inspect the Bailey Building & Loan in the old Frank Capra movie *It's a Wonderful Life.* I was hardly George Bailey, the character played by Jimmy Stewart, and it was hardly a matter of a mere $8,000 misplaced by Uncle Billy. If only it had been so easy.

Barton came in boasting that he had already seized five banks, and that he expected the same fate for Citibank. The markets agreed, and our share price dropped from more than $30 a share in early 1990 to a low of $8⅝, its lowest level since the 1960s. Some of our debt had been reduced to junk-bond status. We needed a "satisfactory" grade on our audit or the federal government could take over the bank and replace its management. The rumor was that Paul Volcker, the former chairman of the Federal Reserve, would be put in charge.

Had we been a typical bank, he'd have been right. No bank had ever come back from the amount of bad credit we held at that time, Barton had said.

But we had a surprise in store for the regulators. I had recently been appointed senior risk officer as of the end of September. Reed had asked me to step in and take over the discussion with the comptroller, which I did after returning from the annual International Monetary Fund (IMF)–World Bank meeting in Bangkok in mid-October.

I immediately plunged in, assembling an internal risk team to go over every single loan in our portfolios, loan by loan. With our chief accountant, a knowledgeable and able Welshman named Tom Jones, we stayed until midnight almost every night and worked on weekends as well—a pace that the Washington staff of that time was unaccustomed to.

In the last quarter, we took massive write-offs—for the year 1991, a total of $736 million in bad property loans from a commercial real estate portfolio of $13 billion, 5.7 percent of our total loans outstanding. Nearly 43 percent of the loans we wrote off were ultimately classified as nonperforming. I promised the same pace of write-offs for the first quarter of the following year. We ended up writing off a then shocking $1.4 billion in 1992.

Historically, we had an aggressive strategy of writing off our bad loans. We continued that strategy, as well as an aggressive recognition of potential problems, classifying loans as impaired based on danger signals alone—long before they could be categorized as nonperforming.

Most banks were relatively slow to take write-offs on their bad loans. Instead, they put money into reserves against the write-offs for when they had to take them. That made their balance sheets look better, but in fact it made those banks weaker. If you take write-offs more aggressively, your balance sheet looks worse, because the reserves won't be as high. But the truth is, you're a healthier organization.

In those days of accounting, if you had a $100 million loan and you thought that all you would get back was $40 million, you wrote off $60 million. If you got back more, it was income.

If you decided to solve the problem with reserves instead, as many banks did, you left the loan on the books as a $100 million asset, but you took $60 million from your income and put it into reserves. When the regulators came in to look at the books, they would say, "This loan isn't worth $100 million," and the banks would say, "Yes, but see, we allocated $60 million in reserves to cover the loss." That way, their books had a $100 million asset, plus an additional $60 million in reserves—leaving both sides on the books. It made these banks look stronger only because people who weren't knowledgeable thought that bigger reserves meant stronger banks. But the reserves were bigger only because the banks hadn't taken the write-offs they should have taken. They were not stronger; they were weaker.

Our approach was ultimately accepted by the regulators, but they didn't believe us at first. Barton thought we were just like the average bank, and that our reserves were too low. He forced us to make a small increase in the reserves in order to make the bank look healthier, but it was minuscule.

Our point was that we were already aggressively writing off the bad loans and therefore we didn't need to make a dramatic increase in our reserves.

That way, the money we received on loans that had been written off or written down—but in fact were still paying interest and principal, even delinquently—was much higher than at most banks. We put any ongoing payments that we received on bad loans toward principal, not income. It was the most conservative way of looking at a bad loan portfolio. As a result, we had a high rate of recovery, between 6 percent and 7 percent. For most banks, it was 2 to 3 percent. We were getting cash in on the loans that we had written off, and that was the key to the regulators believing that we were doing it differently.

During this period, we made changes in our personnel and risk-management processes. We put more authority into the hands of our credit officers, but at the same time increased their contact with top management when there were exceptional loans or portfolio issues to be considered. We gave them more flexibility to lend to borrowers who were deemed to be low risk, and made high-risk loans the subject of high-level attention.

We instituted modeling to derive limits for concentrations of loans by country, industry, and borrower to help us avoid similar problems in the future. Using data from 20 years of defaults and losses, we analyzed the size and location of losses—the "lumps"—to measure performance and smooth out the concentrations. The result was a set of guidelines with which to make future credit decisions, taking the concentrations of risk into account. Previously, talented individual credit officers could be undone by poor controls elsewhere. I wanted to change that.

Later we implemented Windows on Risk (see Lesson 2), an entirely new risk evaluation structure and process designed to identify pending problems. Later I led this process, which was successful in averting a serious problem for Citibank in the next crisis, the Asian financial crisis of 1997–1998.

But in the meantime, we had the current crisis to resolve.

On December 23, 1991, we finally got our report from the regulators.

It read: "Satisfactory."

I immediately called John Reed in our Stamford, Connecticut, office and told him the news. He could hardly believe it. The comptroller's office didn't plan to put out a statement, I said, but we should do it in order to calm the markets, which would be closing for the Christmas holiday. "You do it," Reed said. I put out the statement.

Citibank ultimately wrote off $4 billion over the 18-month period of the real estate crisis. We took big hits on our books, but we didn't sell the real estate portfolio at big discounts, instead waiting on a property-by-property basis for when prices were more realistic.

In the end, through the execution of sound banking judgment and relentless, night-and-day work, we managed Citibank's way out of the crisis.

"CRITICAL MASS"

On November 16, 1982, the president of the Federal Reserve Bank of New York, Tony Solomon, called an emergency meeting. Our CEO, Walter Wriston, phoned me—I was taking a few days off in Saint Martin at the time—and said that the IMF's managing director, Jacques de Larosière, would be discussing the Mexican debt crisis, and that, as the head of Mexico's restructuring committee, I had to be there.

The CEOs of all the major Japanese, Canadian, European, and U.S. banks would be attending. Wriston said that he was sending the Citibank corporate jet to pick me up, and that I needed to be ready and waiting at the airport a few hours later. The meeting would start at 4:30 p.m. in the New York Fed boardroom.

The reason was that in September, following the August blockbuster announcement by Mexico that it could not make its foreign debt payments (see Lesson 4), I had been named the head of the committee to restructure Mexico's debt (see Lesson 7). Such committees, generally made up of about a dozen banks, negotiated on behalf of the hundreds (sometimes up to 1,000) of creditor banks that were owed money.

It was clear that without coordinated action on the part of the banks and the official sector, it was possible that a wave of defaults could destabilize the global banking system and throw the entire world into a depression. Millions would be put out of work, and poverty indexes, which we were endeavoring to lower through loans aimed at helping Latin American economies to develop, would end up rising instead. I knew that we in the private sector would have to act in conjunction with government agencies and the international financial institutions to resolve the crisis.

What began in August 1982 as the "debt bomb" became an international financial crisis without precedent. Along with the social and political impact felt by hundreds of millions of people in the developing world, it resulted in profound changes in the business of international banking.

In hindsight, it may be tempting to feel that the crisis was exaggerated. After all, the international lending system did not collapse, and the Latin American countries eventually were able to return to the international capital markets. But the crisis was real. By the time it had peaked, nearly every country in Latin America—and a number outside the region as well—had been involved. As of the end of 1983, according to the IMF, 30 developing countries were refinancing their debt. The total came to $400 billion by the end of that year, or more than half of all developing country debt. Most of this involved postponing principal payments that were falling due over the coming months, pushing off the immediate problem and requiring a longer-term solution.

Mexico's outstanding debt—never mind that of the succession of countries that quickly followed, including Argentina and Brazil—accounted for 44 percent of the total capital of the nine largest U.S. banks, and the crisis came at a time when creditors were ill prepared to cope with it.

Mexico alone was enough to call into question the capital adequacy ratios of the world's leading lenders.

Given the stakes, we had to assume that the crisis could be managed. Our goal was twofold: first, prevent the collapse of the international financial system and, obviously, the banking system; and second, help the countries eventually return to the private capital markets in order to finance sustained growth in their economies.

The debt restructuring process spawned a number of financial innovations (see Lesson 8). Many of the modern debt management techniques and financial instruments that we now take for granted began during those stormy days.

At first, it seemed that the debtor countries simply lacked liquidity. Thus, our first goal was to assemble emergency short-term financing to stabilize the situation. It soon became clear, however, that the problem was more fundamental. Developing countries in Latin America needed to reform their economies through privatization, revamped trade and tax regulations, and the development of their domestic capital markets and institutions. Without that, the goals of economic development and improved living standards would remain elusive.

In 1982, the United States was in a recession. Federal Reserve Chairman Paul Volcker, in an effort to put the brakes on U.S. inflation, had raised interest rates above 20 percent. The side effect was a global economic downturn.

In the decade leading up to the crisis, most Latin American countries had closed economies, often run by their militaries and all with overgrown public sectors. In the 1970s, when the first oil shock hit, they were willing to borrow heavily in an attempt to keep growth going.

International banks, loaded with an unprecedented flow of petrodollar deposits, saw what appeared to be a commercial opportunity in "recycling" this money to developing countries, namely those in Latin America, in the form of loans. The official sector was doing little, leaving a vacuum that was filled by private-sector lending.

But by the end of the 1970s, inflation in Latin America had risen, and fluctuating interest rates were hitting the countries hard. The combination of the global economic slowdown and skyrocketing interest rates devastated the ability of many developing nations, particularly those in Latin America, to meet their debt obligations. Countries that had borrowed money at floating interest rates needed even more money to pay down the interest on their debts. They also needed time to restructure and put in place reforms that would privatize and open their markets, thereby ensuring a future channel for investment and growth.

So at that IMF-convened meeting in November 1982 at the New York Fed, de Larosière began by highlighting all these points. He then came to the bottom line: in the coming year, Mexico was going to have $10 billion in interest payments due on public-sector debt alone. It faced a current-account deficit of $4.5 billion, as well as $2.5 billion in payments on short-term loans arranged for it at the start of the crisis in August by the Bank for International Settlements (BIS), which is the central bank for central banks. Then, Mexico's official reserves would require $1.5 billion. With a need of $8.3 billion, the magnitude of the Mexican restructuring was unprecedented. The maximum that the IMF was able to provide in those days was $1.3 billion per year. The remainder would have to come from elsewhere.

Other countries providing bilateral aid could be expected to fund the $2 billion.

But that left a hole of $5 billion. The commercial banks would have to come up with it, de Larosière said, providing new loans for Mexico in that amount while also agreeing to restructure the loans that were coming due. They had to do their fair share to help Mexico's recovery. He asked banks to commit in writing to the $5 billion in "new money" for 1983, a rollover of short-term loans, and a long-term debt rescheduling. He said that eventually we would have to do the same kind of new money arrangement for Argentina.

Such written commitments were unprecedented. The goal was to give all the banks a stake in the success of Mexico's restructuring process, and thereby stabilize Mexico and the global economy.

De Larosière said: "I'm going to go ahead with the IMF loans. But I have to be able to say that the banks will be able to put in this new money."

All eyes in the room turned to me. As the head of Mexico's restructuring committee—or Advisory Committee, as we had decided to call it (see Lesson 8)—a huge task had fallen into my lap. Could we pull it off?

We agreed that I would see to it. De Larosière said that he wouldn't be able to disburse loans to Mexico until the commercial banks committed to do it. At that point, he left the room and turned over the meeting to me.

The first step was getting consensus in the room, then within the committee, on how to persuade banks around the world to commit to providing this new money.

It was clear that cooperation was in everyone's interest. But there were some banks—the very small ones that were holding only a small amount of Mexico's debt—that might see it as being in their interests to hold out, not provide new money, and work on getting their money back on their own terms rather than being represented by the restructuring committee. If these so-called free riders didn't go along with putting in new money, getting a commitment from the remaining banks could prove all the more difficult.

Some of the banks were concerned that regulators would look critically at banks increasing their lending to risky countries. Later, Volcker assured us that they would not. His statements once again underlined the necessity of private-sector and official-sector cooperation.

De Larosière initially wanted each creditor bank to increase its exposure by 9 percent of what it was owed. This was considered a large enough amount so that if small banks declined, the $5 billion could still be raised.

On November 30, I met with him in his office in Washington, D.C., and told him that if small banks realized that they weren't necessary to reach the goal, they wouldn't participate at all. The number had to be low enough that, upon calculation, all banks would realize that they must participate. I suggested 5 percent.

Our compromise was the obvious one: 7 percent. We started calling it the "7 percent solution." At that rate, more than 500 banks would have to participate, and only a few could be let off the hook.

The problem was that the money needed to be raised by the IMF-set deadline of December 25, and it was going to be virtually impossible to get all the banks to agree and to pledge their money in time. The 25 largest creditors would provide just $2 billion—that was easy enough; the next $2 billion would come from 75 smaller banks. But the final $1 billion would require pulling in more than 400 institutions around the world. It was a Herculean task.

We decided that if a large enough percentage of the banks—a "critical mass"—went along by the end of the year, we could move forward and the IMF could trigger its disbursements. De Larosière wanted 90 percent of the banks' participation to constitute critical mass. I said that the banks on the Advisory Committee thought the maximum we could get on board was 70 percent. We agreed on 80 percent. But in the end we got more than that.

It was not without a last-minute struggle, however. By December 23, we had commitments for only $4.3 billion. We were $700 million short. Banks in Switzerland, France, Japan, and Britain, as well as some regional banks in the United States, were holding out. We needed a final push to bring the rest on board. We sent members of the Advisory Committee along with a senior Mexican official, José Angel Gurría, now head of the OECD, to visit the world's capitals, particularly Tokyo and those in the Middle East, to bring about the consensus. Once the IMF was confident that the critical mass had been reached, it moved forward.

"Critical mass," adjusted case by case, would be the mantra of debt restructuring for the next decade.

On March 15, 1983, the last 7 of 526 creditor banks signed on, giving us the $5 billion that I had promised the IMF we could raise. The first phase of the debt crisis was over, and our relentless pursuit of a solution and coordination of the private and public sectors had paid off.

ARGENTINA: THE BRADY PLAN

In early 1992, it again became apparent that an attitude of determined relentlessness pays off. I was chairing the "Working Group" made up of 13 international banking institutions and the Argentine government, trying to finalize a $31 billion Brady bond deal (so named because the bonds were pioneered by Treasury Secretary Nicholas Brady) for Argentina to restructure its debt.

When it came time to push for a final agreement to resolve an impasse, I insisted that everyone involved remain at the negotiating table all night long, for two nights in a row, to get it done. The result was the fastest-yet negotiating time for a major international debt restructuring.

Argentina's economy was only just starting to recover from its terrible shocks of the 1980s. When President Carlos Menem took office in 1989, the economy was in a critical state, with $65 billion of external debt, skyrocketing hyperinflation of over 5,000 percent annually, and a serious economic contraction. Menem had appointed the former head of the Central Bank, Domingo Cavallo, to be minister of the economy and to try to stabilize the economy through trade liberalization, deregulation, and privatization.

In April 1991, Cavallo had implemented a radical monetary reform plan called "Convertibility," which pegged the new Argentine peso to the U.S. dollar at a rate of $1 = 1 peso and limited the growth in the money supply to the growth in reserves. Initially, it worked. Inflation fell to single digits, and economic growth rebounded. Next, Argentina had to pay its creditors.

There was hope that the Brady plan was going to put an end to Latin America's economic troubles and finally halt the region's constant cycle of debt restructuring (see Lesson 8).

We kicked off our talks at a meeting in New York on January 30, 1992. It soon became clear that the Argentines and the international banking community were very far apart. The banks wanted a large cash payment from Argentina to cover about $10 billion in past-due interest payments on existing loans. This situation was unique to Argentina—when we negotiated the first Brady bond deal with Mexico, past-due interest was not an issue because Mexico had always kept current with its interest payments. The banks also wanted Argentina's commitment to make monthly payments "in a significant amount." The number put forward was $1.1 billion.

The Argentines wanted nothing of the sort. They proposed making modest payments each month, not a large cash payment. They offered far less, with lower interest payments, which the banks would not agree to.

Talks dragged on through February and March. By April, the two sides were still more than $1 billion apart. We were at an impasse.

Pressure was coming from the U.S. Treasury, which was anxious to see a deal for Argentina in order to ensure stability, and also to see the second successful completion of Brady bonds. The Argentines had a newly negotiated $3.6 billion multiyear program with the IMF that required successful resolution of commercial bank debt as a condition of loan disbursements as well. We needed to reach an agreement.

The annual meeting of the Inter-American Development Bank (IDB) was scheduled for Santo Domingo, the capital of the Dominican Republic, on April 6–8, 1992. All the major parties were going to be there: the IMF, the World Bank, the major banks, and the governments. Unlike negotiations in New York, which could drag on interminably, the IDB meeting was for a finite period—just three days in all, beginning Monday morning. We had a built-in deadline.

Everyone going down to the meeting knew that discussions to try to finalize the deal were going to take place on the sidelines. But they had no idea what they were in for.

My team and I decided that we were going to force the issue and make it happen there and then, before the IDB meeting adjourned. We had just 36 hours. We planned it like a campaign—we decided that we were not going to let people leave the conference room, except to eat and go to the bathroom, until we had reached a deal. If we let the negotiations drag on back in New York, the impetus to get the deal done would disappear. We needed closure.

The IDB events started Saturday evening with a reception at the InterContinental Hotel, a downtown high-rise hotel, hosted by Scotiabank. Our team went around the room collecting people, notifying everyone that negotiations would begin that evening at 8 p.m., immediately after cocktails, at an outside hotel some distance away, where we had secured a conference room.

"You can bring your drinks," I told them. I knew we were going to be in for a long session, but nobody on the 13-member committee knew what was in store for them.

It wasn't much of a hotel. All the higher-end hotels in Santo Domingo were booked because of the IDB meeting.

We couldn't use the conference rooms at the InterContinental because word might leak to the press and scuttle the negotiations.

The conference room at our secluded location was hot, windowless, and dank. We needed the air conditioner, but when it was on, you couldn't hear people speak. We kept having to shut it off, raising the temperature not only of the room but of the participants as well.

The "business center" consisted of a fax machine; it had no computers on which to update term sheets and the ongoing progress of negotiations. To implement the changes as they were agreed to, our lawyer from Shearman & Sterling, Jeanne Olivier, who played a key role in the process, had to fax hand-marked documents to an associate back in New York, who inserted the comments into the term sheet and faxed them back to Santo Domingo.

At one point during the night, the documents that were faxed back from New York got locked in the business center—we could see them through the glass, but we could not get to them until we could locate someone at the hotel with a key. Then the fax ran out of toner, and committee participants complained that they couldn't read the documents on which decisions involving billions of dollars were riding.

The odd thing about debt negotiations is that very little actually gets decided in the room itself. Much is worked out in the corridors and hallways, and by phone between the parties. Preagreements in corridors are the norm, and then everyone comes back into the room to give a verdict on the particular term sheet that is on the table at the time.

As was my habit, I was relentless in repeatedly going around the table and making everyone openly declare a position or come up with a solution (see Lesson 8). Intermediaries such as Terry Checki, the Federal Reserve Bank of New York's international troubleshooter, were running up and down the stairs, trying to find consensus. It was a pressure cooker. Occasionally we ended up at the kitchen table of a suite at the hotel rented by the Argentine delegation.

We did this all night Saturday night, then all through the day again on Sunday. People were exhausted, ready to drop. Most participants didn't have rooms to stay in at that little Santo Domingo hotel. In order to sleep or freshen up, they would have had to go back to the InterContinental or somewhere else, wherever they had booked a room for the event. I insisted that they stay. People were napping amidst pizza boxes on chairs in the hallways, and drinking cup after cup of coffee.

By Sunday night, you got the feeling that the participants would have said yes to almost anything just to be able to go to bed. That, I knew, was when we could make the most progress. Nobody was to leave until we were finished.

Because we were at a public event at which expectations were high and the media were in attendance awaiting an announcement, we could not afford to fail. It was a high-risk gamble, but I knew we could get it done by forcing the issue and persisting with determined relentlessness.

Very early on Monday morning, close to 5 a.m., we finally reached an agreement in principle. Everyone was so worn out that we were just running on adrenaline. We adjourned, went back to the InterContinental to take showers, then reassembled for a 10 a.m. press conference at which the deal was announced.

In the end, it was the fastest negotiation yet of a debt restructuring—just 69 days from our start on January 30 (it was a leap year). The agreement covered $23 billion in medium-term debt and $8 billion in arrears on interest payments.

Under the terms of the Brady deal, banks could choose to forgive 35 percent of their loans in exchange for a floating-rate security for the value of the remaining 65 percent, collateralized by U.S. Treasury bonds. Or, they could swap their loans for bonds, also backed by U.S. Treasury bonds, that maintained the face value of the loans but carried a fixed interest rate below market levels. In addition, banks were permitted to continue to exchange their loans for shares in various Argentine companies that were being privatized.

Argentina, in exchange, agreed to pay $400 million in cash and $300 million in short-term securities on the overdue interest, and issue uncollateralized, 12-year Argentine bonds for the remaining unpaid interest. It also agreed to pay $70 million per month in interest on other obligations.

At the press conference, in front of the Argentine delegation and the full Working Group, Argentina's Finance Minister Cavallo and I made statements.

I said that the agreement "improves the relationship between the country and its commercial bank creditors; it allows the country to have greater access to the international voluntary capital markets and—when fully implemented—it will enable Argentina to put the debt crisis behind it."

In a phone interview with the *New York Times* before I left Santo Domingo, I said: "With this agreement, we are looking at the end of the LDC debt crisis" because we were about to begin negotiating with Brazil.

Cavallo said that he expected total foreign debt to decrease by $10 billion as a result of the agreement. "It will allow Argentina to recover confidence in its future—a confidence that had been lacking at times in the past. I am sure that this agreement will mean a turning point in the Argentina economy."

Well, until the next Argentine crisis a decade later.

———

To GET A DEAL DONE or to pass a regulator's audit, the same method applies: you need to be persistent. You need to keep everyone involved glued to the goal of a project's final completion, even when they want to leave the negotiating table. Skip sleep if necessary. Get it done. You also need to coordinate with the official sector and any stakeholders in the process to head off any possible opposition to getting a deal done as quickly as possible. Time is your enemy. Conquer it; control it.

BIBLIOGRAPHY

COMPTROLLER OF THE CURRENCY

"No Small Change." *The Economist,* April 10, 1993.

Zuckerman, Laurence. "Run on Citibank-Hong Kong." *New York Times,* August 9, 1991.

Zweig, Phillip L. *Wriston: Walter Wriston, Citibank, and the Rise and Fall of American Supremacy.* New York: Crown Publishers, 1996, Chapter 26.

———

"Critical Mass"

Boughton, James M. *Silent Revolution: The International Monetary Fund, 1979–1989.* Washington, D.C.: International Monetary Fund, 2001, pp. 306–317.

Rhodes, William R. "LDC Debt Policy, 3." In Martin Feldstein (ed.) *American Economic Policy in the 1980s.* Chicago and London: National Bureau of Economic Research, 1994, pp. 725–739.

Rhodes, William R. "A Very Real Crisis." *International Financing Review,* October 8, 1993.

Argentina

Lipin, Steven. "Foreign Banks and Argentina Set Debt Accord." *Wall Street Journal,* April 8, 1992.

Quint, Michael. "Argentina Reaches Pact to Cut Debt." *New York Times,* April 8, 1992, pp. D1, D5.

TAKE PROMPT, COMPREHENSIVE ACTION

Tracking Down Mexico's Finance Minister,
Getting Brazil to Restructure Its Debt, and
Managing South Korea's Financial Crisis
and Its Free Trade Pact

Sometimes you just have to get on a plane and go. Getting right to the heart of the problem is critical when time is of the essence. Insisting on an answer, even when you have to fly to another country to get it, can make all the difference when you are faced with a critical situation.

I had to do this when the finance minister in charge of Mexico's debt restructuring disappeared for more than a week at the height of our debt restructuring talks during the Latin American debt crisis of the 1980s. After leaving countless messages and not hearing back, I decided to get on a plane for Mexico City. Upon arriving, I left word at his office and home that I wasn't going anywhere until I knew what had happened to him. For Brazil the following year, getting to the heart of the matter meant hopping on a plane to Brasília to convince the Brazilians that they needed to go along with conditions set by the International Monetary Fund for a relief package so that we bankers could finish a debt restructuring to deal with the debt crisis. More than a decade later, it also meant jumping on a plane to South Korea to find out whether the newly elected president was prepared to go along with our debt restructuring, which led South Korea out of the depths of the Asian financial crisis of 1997. That move, along with working the phones to Japan into the wee hours of the night, allowed me and my fellow bankers to get our colleagues around the world on board with South Korea's restructuring deal. Later, I urged the U.S. government to work toward a free trade agreement between the two countries.

The lesson here is that it's never over till it's over. Take action when it's needed. Just get on a plane or pick up the phone and get to the heart of the matter.

MEXICO: TRACKING DOWN JESÚS SILVA HERZOG

It was like Stanley looking for Livingstone, only it wasn't Africa—it was in the middle of Mexico City. During a crucial stage of negotiations with Mexico during its debt crisis in 1982, the minister of finance, Jesús Silva Herzog, disappeared for more than a week. I decided to go and find him.

Silva Herzog was a charismatic, Yale University–educated economist, and the son of one of Mexico's great intellectuals and politicians. Universally he was known to English speakers by his nickname, "Chucho," because, as someone once explained, as great as he was, it was still hard to call him "Jesus."

By early 1982, Mexico held $80 billion in foreign debt, a third of it owed to U.S. banks. After a devaluation of the currency, capital was fleeing the country as the wealthy sought to convert pesos to dollars and move them into safer locales overseas. President José López Portillo had pledged to defend the value of the peso "like a dog," a remark that led his detractors to call him *El Perro* (the dog) when he devalued it anyway. The devaluation, and his unsustainable pledge to uphold the peso, led Mexican crowds to jeer, boo, and even bark like dogs during his public appearances. They called the luxury mansion that he built on a hill outside Mexico City after he left office the *Colina del Perro*, or Dog Hill.

Unemployment had reached 13 percent, and inflation was 60 percent annually. High U.S. dollar interest rates of over 20 percent had pushed up the interest payments that Mexico owed on its foreign debt. It was clear that Mexico needed debt relief.

A failure by Mexico to repay would have had implications far beyond the country's borders: American banks' exposure to Mexico was substantial. Total Mexican debt nearly equaled the capital of the nine largest U.S. banks. And banks as far away as Saudi Arabia and Tokyo were also holding Mexican paper. The fear in the market was that a Mexican default could take down a few venerable banking institutions, including Bank of America, Citibank, Chase, Manufacturers Hanover, Chemical Bank (the previous two now part of JPMorgan Chase), and international banks in Europe and Japan as well.

Talk among officials in Mexico City was that the country might need an emergency bailout from the International Monetary Fund (IMF), despite the austerity measures that always accompanied it. But there was an election coming up in Mexico on July 4. Even though the Institutional Revolutionary Party (PRI) was politically strong and had ruled Mexico for most of the twentieth century, López Portillo did not think it expedient to implement harsh austerity, such as cutting government spending and wages (which he had raised following the peso's devaluation). IMF measures would impose more hardships on the Mexican people and potentially weaken the PRI's power base. López Portillo could not run again, but his anointed successor, Miguel de la Madrid—who later turned out to be Mexico's first market-oriented president—still needed to shore up public support.

Silva Herzog put in place some of the more palatable programs to reduce the balance of payments deficit by instituting import controls and to restore confidence in the falling peso. He proposed cutting the budget deficit by 8.3 percent by curtailing government spending and raising the prices of electricity, gasoline, and other goods and services provided by the government.

Then in April, he went directly to the U.S. Federal Reserve, in its capacity as lender of last resort, and arranged with Federal Reserve Chairman Paul Volcker for a currency swap of $600 million. It actually worked like a bridge loan: the Fed deposited the money in Mexico's account at the New York Fed in exchange for pesos.

Since international debt servicing required payment in dollars, this was enough to keep the Mexican economy afloat and prevent it from showing an end-of-month depletion of reserves. When the money was repaid, Mexico got $200 million at the end of June and another $700 million at the end of July. The swaps were secret; they had to be reported only every quarter, and Volcker hoped that by the end of the quarter, Mexico would be back on solid footing, the election would be over, and Mexico could then negotiate with the IMF for help in exchange for fiscal discipline.

But by August, billions of dollars in foreign debt were coming due. On August 12, 1982, Silva Herzog placed separate phone calls to Volcker; the U.S. secretary of the Treasury, Donald Regan; and the managing director of the IMF, Jacques de Larosière. He said that the money from the swaps had been depleted. Mexico had nearly run out of reserves, and the country needed help. He and José Angel Gurría, the young head of external finance, plus a few other Mexican officials, flew to Washington that evening.

After a series of negotiations for more emergency funds in Washington, Silva Herzog returned to Mexico and then made plans to come to New York for meetings with Mexico's principal creditor banks on August 19.

I was in Quebec that week, and I got a call from the office of our CEO, Walter Wriston, who had received a personal phone call from Silva Herzog explaining the situation and requesting to meet with creditors. Wriston's office immediately phoned me.

"The Mexicans are in trouble," I was told. I hurried home.

Mexico's crisis was the beginning of what would come to be called the "debt bomb." It may seem commonplace now, but a major country's inability to meet debt payments was unprecedented at the time. The world hadn't had such a shock since the Great Depression of the late 1920s and 1930s. There were no blueprints for dealing with such a situation. We had to draw them up as we went along.

In hindsight this may have been a blessing in disguise. With bad news from Argentina and Brazil soon to follow, we had to develop a formula for handling a crisis of this magnitude. First, we had to assume that the crisis could be managed. Then, to contain any panic, we had to convince the world financial community that we could manage it. After that, we needed to work with the governments involved to get them on board and convince their people that some of the tough measures that needed to be taken in order to stabilize their economies would in fact eventually return them to growth, higher employment, and more efficient economies. I knew then that the process was going to take years, if not decades.

Silva Herzog—starting with one-on-one meetings with top New York bankers, followed by meetings at the New York Fed the next morning—asked for a voluntary postponement of $10 billion in principal payments. As near as anyone could tell, somewhere between 500 and 1,000 banks held Mexican debt. Of the 800 creditor banks that had been invited to the meeting, 115 had sent representatives to hear Silva Herzog's request.

The Mexicans, after consulting with Volcker, asked that representatives of Citibank and Bank of America co-chair the Advisory Committee. Because of my previous experience with rescheduling the debts of Nicaragua and Jamaica, and because I knew the Mexican players, I was made principal co-chair (see Lesson 7). Later that afternoon, we began negotiations at Citibank headquarters on

Park Avenue. Fourteen banks—Chase, Chemical, Morgan Guaranty, Bank of America, Bankers Trust, Manufacturers Hanover, Bank of Tokyo, Lloyds, Société Générale, Bank of Montreal, Swiss Bank Corp., Deutsche Bank, and Banamex of Mexico, as well as Citibank—attended as representatives of all the creditor banks.

The first thing we did was get the banks to stop pulling their trade and interbank lines. Subsequently, our first negotiation was to arrange several hundred million dollars in new money, and then later to embark on restructuring the debt after agreements with the IMF had been reached.

Nearly a month of negotiations was proving fruitful. We agreed to postpone principal payments covering the $10 billion that was due between August 23 and November 23 for 90 days, with the proviso that Mexico then agree to austerity and reform measures under the IMF in exchange for new loans. The peso, which had been valued at 26 pesos = $1 before devaluation, had fallen to 120, before stabilizing at around 80 = $1 after the announcement. Next, we were moving on to discussing new financing.

In the meantime, however, on September 1, López Portillo had sent more shocks through the international financial community. The election had already been held, and López Portillo was a lame duck giving his last state-of-the-nation address. Yet he ordered the nationalization of 49 domestic banks in Mexico and the imposition of exchange controls, further spooking the markets. The president had accused the banks of being involved in a massive "looting" of the nation and said that his actions were necessary to halt further capital flight and speculation in the peso.

Because the Mexicans, and Silva Herzog in particular, appreciated the lead institutional role that Citibank was taking in chairing the restructuring process, as the only foreign bank with branch operations in Mexico, we were spared nationalization. I pointed out to Silva Herzog that it would be difficult for us to keep chairing the committee if we were nationalized, and besides, we had a minuscule share of the market—less than one-half of 1 percent.

Silva Herzog tried to resign along with the heads of the central bank and the foreign trade bank. But López Portillo refused only Silva Herzog's resignation. Silva Herzog then tried to limit the impact of the nationalization by influencing the selection of the government officials appointed to oversee the nationalized banks. The nationalization left the government responsible for another $10 billion in foreign debt owed by the nationalized Mexican banks.

But then suddenly, at a crucial stage in our negotiations, Silva Herzog disappeared. During a meeting in New York on September 23, Angel Gurría had brought a fresh batch of economic data prepared by the ministry of finance and confirmed that negotiations with the IMF were ongoing.

The point under discussion was that Mexico would continue to pay out both interest and principal on its loans and service its bonds subject to the renegotiation, provided we came up with new money, kept interbank lines alive, and lengthened the payments on principal. But before proceeding further, we wanted reassurances from Silva Herzog himself that Mexico would live up to such a deal.

Yet Silva Herzog could not be reached. I phoned Mexico City numerous times and left messages with his office, which would not explain his whereabouts. Nor would Angel Gurría during our sessions in New York. I phoned his home. He was not there. We were very close to getting a deal done, and he was the key. I knew that he didn't want to default, and that he wanted to work out a restructuring. But I couldn't figure out what was going on.

I started becoming concerned that something had happened to him, either politically or physically or both. In addition, international banks started worrying that Mexico might default. At our banking committee meetings in New York, the representatives of the world's banks wanted answers. Silva Herzog was the man who symbolized Mexico's ability to work its way out of this crisis. He was the key to Mexican economic stability and our link to making sure that Mexico would negotiate proper terms with the IMF. Yes, we had Angel Gurría, but at the time he was a junior official, and he wasn't telling us anything.

We had come to trust Silva Herzog, yet nobody could explain why he had disappeared. Without him, that trust was on the verge of vanishing. The members of the banking committee were getting antsy. They threatened to end the negotiations and go home.

So on September 29, I got on a plane and flew to Mexico. I phoned Silva Herzog's office. I left a message. I phoned his home. I left a message. When he didn't call back, I phoned again. I left word everywhere that I had come to Mexico City, I had checked into the Camino Real hotel, and I was not going to leave until I had an explanation.

Finally, a couple of days later, while I was having lunch in the hotel, I got a call from him.

"What's going on? Are you okay?" I asked, frustrated from the long silence and the dozens of unreturned phone calls. Yet, suddenly relieved, I asked him about his health and whether he was still in office.

"I'm alive, and I'm still minister," he said. But he revealed that he was in a medical clinic recovering from an operation. He had had appendicitis, but he hadn't wanted anyone to know for fear of the impact on the markets. And he hadn't thought about the implications of his absence for the debt negotiations and how important it would be. He had directed his office and his colleagues not to reveal his whereabouts, and that was what had accounted for their silence.

I immediately phoned New York to inform my colleagues in the banking community.

That act earned Silva Herzog's trust. He realized my dedication to the restructuring process, and that earned his respect. He understood the importance of the need to move on with negotiations, and we did so forthwith.

By December, we had arranged $5 billion in new money for Mexico and had made headway on the restructuring.

There are times when the only option is just to take action, to get on a plane and go. This was one of them. If I hadn't done it, I wouldn't have been able to hold the banks together to work out a deal. That deal—the beginning of the whole restructuring process for Latin America—could have fallen apart, and the impact on the markets would have been enormous. Stanley had finally found Livingstone, and the outcome would postpone Mexico's crises for another day.

BRAZIL

The critical period for Brazil began when Phase 1 of its debt restructuring broke down. A casualty of the Latin

American debt bomb that exploded in 1982, Brazil in 1983 was seeking a relief package. It was divided into four projects, and three had been successfully carried out. The fourth required new credit to replenish interbank lines to Brazil's banks abroad, which had become crucial to keeping Brazil's economy running. But despite support from 180 creditor banks, some U.S. regional banks and some small European ones had declined to restore $9 to $10 billion needed for the interbank lines. So Phase 1 crashed in June 1983.

That's when I was brought in. Our CEO, Walter Wriston, came to my office and said the following:

> I know you're already doing Mexico, Argentina, and Uruguay, but the chairman of the Fed [Paul Volcker] said he also wants you on Brazil. I hate to ask you because you're going night and day on this, but for the good of the system and of the bank, I have to ask you to do this.

He explained that Volcker had said that the system was at risk, and that those who had tried to engineer the first phase for Brazil had hurt Citibank's relationships with other lending institutions. The system needed me, and Citibank needed me, he said.

Phase 2 involved my creating a new advisory committee to carry out a restructuring. We agreed to appoint Guy Huntrods, an executive director of Lloyds Bank International of Britain, and Leighton Coleman of Morgan Guaranty as my vice chairs. Our task was doubly difficult because most of the funds that had been raised in Phase 1 had already been spent. Brazil would need $6.5 billion in new money to make its interest payments on existing loans through the remainder of 1983—plus all of the following year. Rather than raising enough for a small package that would carry Brazil only through the rest of the year, we decided to raise enough money for 1984 as well.

First, I insisted that all banks holding Brazilian debt, however small the amount, participate in the refinancing. I organized the U.S. regional banks into a new coordinating committee so that they couldn't hold out yet again (see Lesson 8). Then Brazil needed to agree to the terms of an IMF package, without which the banks had little appetite for putting in new money to help Brazil.

However, as a result of the failed Phase 1, the head of Brazil's central bank, Carlos Langoni, had concluded that new money to make interest payments wasn't the way to go. He was just 36 years old when he was put into the job in 1980, but he had an impressive string of degrees in economics and had had a distinguished academic career.

He proposed that Brazil be allowed to recapitalize its interest, meaning that the interest due would simply be added to the principal rather than being paid immediately when it was due. He believed that such a move would give the power of decision making back to Brazil instead of keeping it with the banks.

I opposed the idea of capitalizing interest, in part because both the major banks and the U.S. regulators thought that it was a nonstarter. What Brazil needed was cash. Besides, deferring payments just postpones problems into the future. Being forced to make interest payments would impose the kind of fiscal discipline that Brazil would need if it was to resolve its situation. In addition, countries that had capitalized interest payments in the past had had a hard time returning to the credit markets. The time for economic reckoning was now.

A turning point came on August 16, when Huntrods, Coleman, and I got on a private plane and flew to Brasília for an important dinner.

We all agreed that the trip had to be a secret. The Citibank corporate jet that was kept at Teterboro Airport in New Jersey was in for repairs, so we boarded a time-share plane for our nine-hour flight. We timed the trip for immediately after the signing of a $1.5 billion Argentine loan package. We went straight to the airport from the signing at the Argentine consulate on West 56th Street in New York, hoping that the press wouldn't cotton on to the story. We couldn't risk taking a commercial flight, because we didn't want to risk a leak to the press. On the way down, we had plane trouble and had to stop in Barbados for five hours of repairs, but soon we were again on our way. We reached Brasília at 4 a.m. the next day.

The Brazilians said, and I had agreed, that there had better not be any news of our trip in the press. If it appeared, they would deny it. They feared that any leaks would be interpreted as a failure of negotiations, and that their trade and interbank lines would collapse. I didn't want to have to deny it, because that would mean lying to the banks, and I didn't want to lie. I had a reputation for always being clear and completely transparent, explaining the upsides and downsides to all parties. I didn't want to jeopardize that.

The reason for our trip was Brazil's problems with the IMF. Brazil had failed to meet all of the terms for an IMF adjustment program that it had agreed to in February.

In response to the IMF, President João Baptista Figueiredo had increased gas prices 45 percent and started slashing government subsidies for coffee, sugar, and other products, which meant steep price rises for consumers. He cut government spending by $1.2 billion and announced increases in income taxes and new taxes on stock market transactions. Annual inflation soared, as did unemployment. Massive layoffs led to strikes and tens of thousands of protestors in the streets of Rio de Janeiro carrying signs that read "Down with the IMF" and "Moratorium Now." Millions of people living in government housing refused to make their loan payments.

What the IMF wanted next was for Brazil to impose a law saying that wage increases would be limited to 80 percent of the rate of inflation. Although Brazil was reluctant to inflict any more pain on its citizens, President Figueiredo had agreed to introduce the measure to Brazil's Congress. However, his party did not have enough votes to pass it on its own. In fact, opposition politicians were talking about imposing a debt moratorium. The wage cap could become law only if it was not defeated within 60 days—meaning October.

On top of that, the IMF was talking about imposing additional spending restrictions, and a stepped-up reporting by the Brazilian government of its official figures. The IMF was acting tough because it had gotten burned the previous December. It had approved a $4.9 billion loan as part of Phase 1, but it had found that Brazil's government had not gone along with all the measures it had agreed to. As a result, this time the IMF was withholding disbursements of new loans until the measures it had demanded as conditionality were passed into law.

Brazil was using the IMF's refusal to disburse funds as a reason to suspend a $400 million payment on a loan from the Bank for International Settlements (BIS), the central bank for central banks. The payment had been due July 15 and had already been rolled over for 45 days. The Brazilians said that the BIS wouldn't get its money until the IMF disbursed to Brazil what it had pledged. The frustrated BIS president, Fritz Leutwiler, was quoted at the time as saying: "Things just cannot continue as they have been. These [debt] problems will never be solved . . . with money and more money. To say that these [debtor] countries should not be treated with toughness is absolutely grotesque."

We were concerned that if we didn't get the Brazilians to agree to the IMF terms and get its loan disbursement, we couldn't keep trade and interbank lines of credit going. The banks were getting antsy and wanted to see progress. These lines were the lifeline of the Brazilian economy. Without them, the economy could have collapsed, and Brazil would become a financial pariah.

So we arranged to have dinner with Brazil's renowned economist and minister of planning, Antônio Delfim Netto; its finance minister, Ernane Galvêas; and central bank head Langoni. We had agreed to meet at Galvêas's house in Brasília so as not to attract press attention.

Just a year earlier, at the IMF–World Bank annual meeting in Toronto, when Mexico was already falling apart and Argentina was showing signs of serious trouble, Langoni had been confident. None of the troubles of his neighboring countries seemed to worry him, and his country's economic programs were on track. Brazil wasn't Mexico, he said. It would pay its debts. How things had changed.

The world was losing faith in Brazil's economy. Some airlines had canceled flights there because they could not get dollars for their tickets. Royal Dutch/Shell was demanding payments in advance for its oil shipments. There were rumors in the market of default, and local opposition politicians weren't helping by clamoring for a moratorium.

Over our meal, we made the case to the Brazilian officials that they had to go along. I said that unless they reached agreement with the IMF, we wouldn't be able to guarantee their trade and interbank lines of credit. The whole package and all the efforts that had been made so far were going to fall apart, and I wouldn't be able to keep banks from pulling their lines.

"We can't keep the banks on board much longer," I told the Brazilians.

Huntrods chimed in: "There is a smell of defeat around the streets of Brasília that reminds me of France before Dunkirk." The battle of Dunkirk, of course, was the famous World War II battle in 1940 against Nazi Germany where 300,000 Allied troops needed to be rescued after British, French, and Belgian forces seriously underestimated the strength of the German advance, which had cut off nearly all escape routes. Huntrods should know: he had been a lieutenant in the British Navy during the war, and in 1946 he joined the Bank of England as a junior officer before moving to Lloyds in 1975. He also knew Brazil, having been sent by the Bank of England to help set up the central bank of Brazil.

In 1983 the stakes were high for Citibank as well: our Brazil exposure, $4.9 billion, was nearly twice as large as that of any other bank in the world, and amounted to over 80 percent of shareholders' equity that year.

Although we didn't know it at the time, Delfim was just about to leave for Paris for talks with Jacques de Larosière, the IMF's managing director. It turned out that our dinner was fortuitously timed.

Delfim took that message with him to Paris. De Larosière later said that the message was instrumental in getting Brazil to reach an agreement with the IMF. At that meeting, Delfim agreed to take measures that would reduce inflation to 150 percent annually in 1983 and 55 percent annually in 1984, and balance the government budget from a deficit of $15 billion in 1982. The country would increase its trade surplus from $780 million in 1982 to $6 billion in 1983 and $9 billion in 1984. Brazil would report to the IMF once a month, and its lag time for computing official figures would be cut to three weeks.

Langoni, who opposed the toughness of the IMF measures, resigned on September 1. He was replaced by Affonso Celso Pastore, an economics professor at the University of São Paulo. For his handling of the restructuring process, he gained the respect of the financial community both in Brazil and worldwide.

The IMF put Brazil on a stringent monitoring program. It sent a follow-up mission to Brazil every fortnight to check whether the actions the country needed to take were indeed being taken.

There were a number of hurdles and setbacks over the next several months, as Brazil had problems implementing the new wage law until November of that year, which delayed IMF disbursement until then. But we never gave up on the efforts to finalize the deal, and ultimately we raised the $6.5 billion in new money that Brazil needed.

Again, this was a case in which getting on a plane and flying to the heart of the problem—and meeting with the key officials involved to press our point—was what made the difference in Brazil's being able to secure the IMF loan it needed.

SOUTH KOREA: FINANCIAL CRISIS AND FREE TRADE

In the summer of 1997, Asia began to experience the worst financial crisis it had seen in modern history. The crisis started in Thailand in July, when the baht, which had been pegged at 25 to the U.S. dollar, suddenly plunged. The shock came as a surprise to the world, which until then had been witnessing the region's unprecedented growth. Soon the crisis began to spread to South Korea, Indonesia, Malaysia, and the rest of the region. It was clear that the world's financial leaders, including the International Monetary Fund, needed to act to help head off further contagion. An all-out effort got underway to help keep South Korea from defaulting and sending further shocks throughout the region and the world. That's when I got involved.

The highly leveraged *chaebol* conglomerates—Kia Motors, Jinro, Hanbo, Daewoo, and others—which ran everything from trade to manufacturing to services in South Korea, found that they couldn't service the loans that they had taken on in a bid to become some of the biggest companies in the world. Debt-to-equity ratios for the 10 largest *chaebol* exceeded 500 percent, a very high rate of indebtedness. By November, the country's financial institutions were on the verge of defaulting as these *chaebol* became insolvent and found themselves unable to make their loan payments. The government was within days of running out of reserves. The stock market crashed. The won fell by more than half, from $1 = 800 to $1 = 1,700, during the course of the crisis, making things worse.

In November, South Korea went to the International Monetary Fund for a bailout package that would eventually be worth $58 billion. The first tranche was agreed to on December 3, 1997. But the agreement did little to calm the foreign banks, which were still pulling their lines of credit out of South Korea at a rate of hundreds of millions of dollars a day.

By the start of Christmas week, I was on vacation in Barbados, where I got a call from Terry Checki, the man in charge of international issues at the Federal Reserve Bank of New York. The New York Fed was organizing an emergency meeting on South Korea to coordinate the private and public sectors, and he wanted me to fly back to attend.

The IMF and the U.S. Treasury were making emergency loans to South Korea, but they wanted the foreign banks on board to roll over short-term South Korean bank loans that were coming due. All the major European, U.S., and Japanese banks would have to be coordinated in this effort. None of the banks could call its credit lines, and all had to agree not to do so; if there was just one holdout, all the rest of the banks would rush to collect so that they wouldn't be the last ones out. U.S. Deputy Treasury Secretary Lawrence Summers phoned me on Christmas Day to ask for my help.

The Japanese vice minister of finance for international affairs, Eisuke Sakakibara, also phoned me. Known as "Mr. Yen" for his role as Japan's top foreign-exchange policy maker, he said that he had done all he could do to try to convince the Japanese banks. They were South Korea's largest creditors at 40 percent, and they needed assurances that they wouldn't be left holding the bag. Sakakibara was unable to secure such promises himself. He asked me to phone the commercial banks in Japan and ask them to stop pulling out their interbank lines.

Japan no longer worked the way it had in the 1980s, when all that the Ministry of Finance would have had to do was issue a dictum and it would have been followed in all the banking headquarters of Tokyo.

In addition, Japan had been thoroughly rattled by the crisis as well. In November, Sanyo Securities, one of Japan's top 10 brokerage firms, had gone bankrupt with liabilities of more than $3 billion, becoming the first Japanese securities house to go bust since World War II. Then Hokkaido Takushoku Bank, one of Japan's 10 biggest banks, had collapsed under a pile of bad loans. The Japanese banks were in no mood to take risks.

The only way the Japanese banks could be reassured was if I phoned and told them that the American and European banks wouldn't pull their interbank lines. Over the weekend of December 27–28, at home in the evenings and all the way through the New Year's holiday, I worked the phones to Japan. Peter Howell, a Citibank vice president who was the coordinating officer in New York for our Asian businesses, helped me with those calls.

Nights here were mornings there, and we called the heads of all the Japanese banks personally. We reached some of them in the office and some at their homes, but we reached them all—the president, chairman, or vice chairman of every major Japanese bank. Over my years of negotiating in Latin America, I had made many personal contacts in Tokyo. Bank of Tokyo-Mitsubishi was the largest Japanese bank and had the largest overseas operations of any Japanese bank. Tasuku Takagaki, its CEO, and Senior Advisor Toyoo Gyohten (he had been chairman of Bank of Tokyo before the merger with Mitsubishi in 1996) were old friends from years of negotiating Latin American debt. Through the years, we had sat together drinking sake over numerous *kaiseki*, or traditional Japanese multicourse dinners.

The Japanese banks wanted my promise that the Americans and Europeans were also keeping their lines in. I gave them my word. And when I gave them my word, they believed me.

They said, "Do you have their agreement?"

I didn't, in fact, have any such agreement just yet. But I knew that I could pull it off.

"I give you my word," I said.

Then I got on the phone to Europe and did the same.

By December 31, when the South Korean government had to make a payment on loans coming due, its foreign currency reserves had fallen dangerously, to below $10 billion. Rumor had it that at their low point, reserves had fallen below $1 billion. South Korean women were melting down their gold jewelry and donating it to the government to help keep the country from defaulting. The situation was urgent.

We soon put together a committee to restructure South Korea's debt. In early January, South Korea's deputy prime minister and finance minister, Lim Chang-yeul, asked me to chair the debt negotiations.

By January 8, the committee had agreed to a 90-day rollover of roughly $4 billion in loans to South Korea's private sector. But further loan disbursements by the IMF, which had delivered just one-fifth of the promised money, depended on reaching a permanent solution.

We spent the next weeks in tough negotiations around a conference table at our Park Avenue headquarters. By January 28, we had agreed in principle to a plan to exchange $24 billion of South Korea's short-term debt for new loans with longer maturities of up to three years.

But in the meantime there had been an election in South Korea. Kim Dae-jung was elected president just two weeks after the IMF bailout plan was announced. He had been called the Nelson Mandela of Asia for his stance opposing authoritarian rule. A member of the opposition in the National Assembly in the 1960s, Kim had almost been killed after being abducted by the South Korean CIA for criticizing the strongman government that was in power at the time. A U.S. government official intervened to save his life, but he then was imprisoned and banned from politics for many years.

After being sentenced to death—again for criticizing the South Korean government—Kim escaped execution when the U.S. government again intervened and offered him exile in the United States, where he stayed, in Boston and teaching at Harvard, until 1985. After three failed bids for the presidency, he finally won on December 18, 1997, when the public turned against the incumbent government during the economic crisis.

Kim's inauguration marked the first time in South Korean history that the ruling party had peacefully transferred power to a democratically elected opposition candidate. Kim was South Korea's first president to come from a poorer province. In contrast to the conservative government he had defeated, Kim was considered a left-of-center politician.

Yet despite our desire to pull off the agreed-to restructuring, I knew that we couldn't sell a deal until we knew how Kim was going to react—whether he was going to support the IMF package and whether he would abide by the agreements that we were making on short-term debt.

The only way I could find out firsthand was to get on an airplane. A week before his inauguration, I decided to fly to Seoul. Upon my arrival, I was able to schedule a meeting with him for February 20, five days before he was to be inaugurated.

Meeting in his party headquarters office, I told him that banks around the world were prepared to support South Korea if he would just give his assurance that he would accept the tough austerity measures imposed by the IMF as a condition of its bailout loans and abide by the debt restructuring agreement we had made at the end of January. He gave me his word and told me that I could reassure the banks to that effect.

After that, I was able to go back to the banks and assure them that South Korea would live up to the IMF plan and our deal to swap short-term for long-term debt. Getting President Kim's personal pledge had been critical. Next, we went on a road show to London, Frankfurt, Tokyo, and Paris to sell the deal.

I had first warned the South Koreans that their economy was in trouble at a meeting of the Asian Development Bank in Fukuoka, Japan, in May 1997. Kang Kyung-shik was the finance minister at the time, and I had told him that I was concerned about overleveraging in the South Korean banking system and that it could blow. He said that the government didn't want to take any strong measures ahead of the election that was coming up, and he blamed currency speculators rather than any endemic problems like the serious overleveraging in the *chaebol* system.

Kang ended up as the first political casualty of the economic crisis, having been fired in November 1997 when the South Korean won fell precipitously and the talk was that South Korea would soon have to go to the IMF for a bailout. But Kang had told the then president, Kim Young-sam—against the advice of the central bank—that there was no need to call in the IMF. For that action, he was later investigated for dereliction of duty in what was widely called a "vendetta" case. After four months in prison without bail, the charges were dismissed, and he was released.

The restructuring paved the way for South Korea's rapid return to the international bond market. By April, the South Korean government had launched a $4 billion offering, led by Salomon Smith Barney and Goldman Sachs. (At the time, Salomon was not yet part of Citicorp, but it would become so after our upcoming merger with Travelers Group, which owned it.) If the loans had not been restructured, Salomon and Goldman Sachs could not have done the bond offering.

Within two years, South Korea had made a startling recovery. South Korea's turnaround, from the edge of default and back to the credit market, was the quickest recovery of the crisis. The stock market during this time, the KOSPI Index, had plummeted to a low of 280 in 1998, but had recovered to 1,000 only a year later.

As I demonstrated with our calls to the CEOs of the Japanese banks and our flying to meet the new president of the South Korean government himself, it pays to go straight to the head of the pack and to the heart of the problem.

———

ANOTHER EXAMPLE OF taking action in South Korea came in mid-2005, when as chairman of the U.S.-Korea Business Council, I pushed the U.S. government to work for a free trade agreement with the country. If I hadn't gotten U.S. Trade Representative Robert Portman to agree to seek the highest level of trade partnership, the agreement would not have happened.

At the time, I was also chairman of the Council of the Americas, and I was in Washington working to get an agreement on CAFTA, the Caribbean Free Trade Agreement. The members of our International Advisory Council and I held a series of meetings with top officials of the U.S. administration, Congress, and the business sector. We were briefed at the White House on the political and security aspects of the U.S.–Latin America/Caribbean relationship by Andrew Card, chief of staff to the president; Stephen Hadley, the national security advisor; Portman, the newly appointed U.S. trade representative; and John Negroponte, the director of national intelligence. Portman also accepted my invitation to speak to us at the U.S.-Korea Business Council a few days later, along with his deputy, Karan Bhatia.

That July, the U.S. Congress approved the U.S.–Central America–Dominican Republic Free Trade Agreement (CAFTA-DR), after nearly three years of efforts on the part of a number of people, including myself and other members of the Council of the Americas.

In my conversation with Portman and Bhatia, I said that in my capacity as the new chairman of the U.S.-Korea Business Council, I had to recommend that, in addition to

CAFTA, we should also pursue such an agreement with our large trading partner, South Korea.

At that meeting, I was told that the U.S. government planned to seek a lower-level trade agreement, known as a trade and investment framework agreement (TIFA), that would not require the highest level of access to markets. I insisted that we work toward the full Monty, a full free trade agreement. The administration didn't think such an agreement could be worked out with South Korea because there were a number of trade disputes going on, including the fact that South Korea continued to ban imports of U.S. beef, ostensibly because of fears over mad cow disease, although U.S. officials considered that reason a pretext.

On January 9, 2006, I wrote an op-ed piece in the *Financial Times* making the case. A free trade agreement would bring major economic benefits to both the United States and South Korea and strengthen one of America's most important allies in the fight against terrorism and in supplying troops to Iraq, I wrote. My op-ed spawned a series of other op-eds in both the English-language and Korean-language press back in Seoul, which then spurred the South Korean side to get on board.

China had just surpassed the United States as South Korea's largest export market, although the United States continued to be the largest source of foreign investment in South Korea, mainly in financial services and manufacturing. I wrote that an agreement would increase two-way flows of trade and investment, giving businesses and consumers access to each other's markets and cheaper goods and services.

I cited a 2004 study by the Institute for International Economics that estimated that U.S. exports to South Korea would rise by 43.2 percent following a free trade agreement, while South Korean exports to the United States would increase by 22.9 percent.

Also, North Korea was a concern. I said that a free trade agreement would help revitalize and strengthen the broader alliance between the United States and South Korea, contributing to the security and stability not only of both countries, but of the Asia-Pacific region as well. It would support further progress in regional and multilateral agreements by addressing many of the challenging issues that were being confronted in trade negotiations at that time.

A failure to negotiate this free trade agreement would be a lost opportunity to facilitate more robust economic activity between the two countries at a time when South Korea's trade and investment flows were becoming increasingly Asia-centric. South Korea was negotiating trade agreements with Japan, the European Union, and India, as well as with other Asian countries. The United States should not be left out.

But attempts to negotiate the free trade agreement were entangled in long-standing U.S. trade grievances. They included South Korea's quota on American films, its restrictions on importing U.S. beef, and the U.S.'s desire for a level playing field for U.S. companies in the automotive, pharmaceutical, and other sectors in South Korea. I wrote that the failure to resolve these issues was an unacceptable barrier to progress in trade relations.

On February 2, the Office of the U.S. Trade Representative (USTR) announced that it would seek to negotiate a free trade agreement with South Korea. Formal talks between the two countries began in Washington, D.C., on June 5.

———

South Korea had a mixed reaction to such a deal. At one point, the discussions were almost derailed when South Korean farmers and other interest groups that were opposed to opening their markets and competing with foreign goods held massive and violent protests in the streets.

So in my capacity as chairman of the U.S.-Korea Business Council, I led a delegation to Seoul to see President Roh Moo-hyun on June 20 at the Blue House (South Korea's equivalent of the White House). The South Korean president's position on the issue of free trade wasn't clear, even though I had urged him to support it the first time we had met, at the Asia-Pacific Economic Cooperation (APEC) meeting in November 2005 in Busan, the large port city on the southern tip of South Korea.

At our meeting in June, representatives from various industries—pharmaceutical, auto, and media—accompanied me. We were scheduled to have only a half hour to urge more access to the South Korean market, but our meeting lasted more than an hour, to the consternation of Roh's Blue House aides.

I met President Roh again on September 13, 2006, when he came to Washington, D.C., to have a summit with President George W. Bush. President Roh addressed a group of business leaders at a lunch cohosted by the U.S.-Korea Business Council and the U.S. Chamber of Commerce. Top executives from 11 major U.S. corporations, including Boeing, General Motors, and MetLife, were also there. At the lunch, the South Korean president assured us of his "strong determination" to conclude a free trade agreement.

Our efforts paid off.

On June 30, 2007, in Washington, the United States and the Republic of Korea signed the United States–Korea Free

Trade Agreement (KORUS FTA). If approved, it would be the United States' most commercially significant free trade agreement in more than 16 years.

The announcement by the USTR when the agreement was signed said that the U.S. International Trade Commission estimated that the reduction of South Korean tariffs and tariff-rate quotas on goods alone would add $10 billion to $12 billion to annual U.S. GDP and around $10 billion to annual merchandise exports to South Korea.

Under the FTA, nearly 95 percent of bilateral trade in consumer and industrial products would become duty free within 3 years of ratification, and most remaining tariffs would be eliminated within 10 years.

For agricultural products, the FTA would immediately eliminate or phase out tariffs and quotas on a broad range of products, with almost two-thirds (by value) of South Korea's agriculture imports from the United States becoming duty free upon ratification.

For services, the FTA would provide meaningful market access commitments that extend across virtually all major service sectors, including greater and more secure access for international delivery services and the opening up of the South Korean market to foreign legal consulting services.

In the area of financial services, the FTA would increase access to the South Korean market and ensure greater transparency and fair treatment for U.S. suppliers of financial services. The FTA would also address nontariff barriers in a wide range of sectors and include strong provisions on competition policy, labor and the environment, and transparency and regulatory due process. The KORUS FTA would also provide U.S. suppliers with greater access to the South Korean government procurement market. And as estimated by the U.S. Chamber of Commerce, if the United States does not implement the agreement, and the EU and Canada trade agreements with South Korea, which have already been approved, become operative (and it is expected that the EU agreement will be in full force by July 2011), nearly $35 billion in U.S. exports will be lost, putting at risk 345,000 American jobs.

At their last meeting in November 2010 in Seoul, at the G-20 meeting, President Obama and Lee Myung-bak, the president of South Korea, reaffirmed the economic and strategic importance of the agreement. President Obama said that he was a "strong believer" in its economic benefits, and the leaders pledged to move forward and work out the remaining issues that were holding up ratification, particularly in the auto sector. I believed this commitment was for real, so I worked with the South Koreans, the White House, and USTR up to the last minute to help achieve this agreement.

On December 3, 2010, negotiations came to an end, and an agreement was finally reached. President Obama stated that the implementation of the agreement will boost exports to South Korea by US$11B and support at least 70,000 new American jobs. It will need to be approved by the elective representative bodies of both countries—the U.S. Congress here and the National Assembly in South Korea. It is my belief that this will probably occur by the end of the second quarter of 2011.

Because of the repeated commitments to this trade deal on both sides of the Pacific, I remain confident of a successful conclusion. You may ask, then, why I have included this as an example of success. I've done so in order to show that it's not over until it's over. You need to persevere, even in the face of setbacks, when the issue is of critical importance.

―――

You can't always solve problems from a desk at headquarters, even by telephone. At times, the only way to get to the heart of the matter and find a solution is to get on an airplane and meet with the key actors involved to press your point and resolve the problem. It doesn't matter whether it is Mexico, Brazil, South Korea, or Wichita, Kansas. The point here is that flying to the epicenter of a problem can make a difference in its resolution.

BIBLIOGRAPHY

Mexico

Coerver, Don M., Suzanne B. Pasztor, and Robert Buffington. *Mexico: An Encyclopedia of Contemporary Culture and History.* Santa Barbara, Calif.: ABC-CLIO, 2004, pp. 46–47.

Greider, William. *Secrets of the Temple: How the Federal Reserve Runs the Country.* New York: Simon & Schuster, 1989, pp. 483–487.

Kraft, Joseph. *The Mexican Rescue.* New York: Group of Thirty, 1984.

"Mexico Alters View on Debt." *New York Times*, September 8, 1982. http://www.nytimes.com/1982/09/08/business/mexico-alters-view-on-debt.html, accessed June 27, 2009.

―――

Riding, Alan. "Man in the News: Survivor: Jesús Silva Herzog." *New York Times*, August 21, 1982. http://www.nytimes.com/ 1982/08/21/business/man-in-the-news-survivor-jesus-silva -herzog.html, accessed June 27, 2009.

Riding, Alan. "Mexico's Economy: Need for Sacrifice Is Stressed." *New York Times*, May 25, 1982. http://www.nytimes.com/ 1982/05/25/business/mexico-s-economy-need-for-sacrifice -is-stressed.html, accessed June 27, 2009.

Solomon, Steven. *The Confidence Game: How Unelected Central Bankers Are Governing the Changed World Economy.* New York: Simon & Schuster, 1995, pp. 205–217.

Zweig, Phillip L. *Wriston: Walter Wriston, Citibank, and the Rise and Fall of American Financial Supremacy.* New York: Crown Publishers, 1995, p. 777.

Brazil

Adam, Nigel. "How They Tried to Rescue Brazil." *Euromoney*, October 1983.

Boughton, James M. *Silent Revolution: The International Monetary Fund, 1979–1989.* Washington, D.C.: International Monetary Fund, 2001, pp. 372–377.

Chernow, Ron. *The House of Morgan: An American Banking Dynasty and the Rise of Modern Finance.* New York: Grove Press, 1990, p. 646.

Glynn, Lenny. "The Field Marshal of the Debt Crisis." *Institutional Investor*, February 1986, pp. 62–72.

Lampert, Hope. *Behind Closed Doors: Wheeling and Dealing in the Banking World.* New York: Athenaeum Press, 1986, pp. 158–189.

Osborn, Neil. "The Rhodes Show Goes On and On." *Euromoney*, March 1984, pp. 33–37.

Solomon, Steven. *The Confidence Game: How Unelected Central Bankers Are Governing the Changed World Economy.* New York: Simon & Schuster, 1995, p. 244.

Zweig, Phillip L. *Wriston: Walter Wriston, Citibank, and the Rise and Fall of American Financial Supremacy.* New York: Crown Publishers, 1995, pp. 784–790.

South Korea

American Business and the Korean Miracle: U.S. Enterprises in Korea, 1866–the Present. Seoul: American Chamber of Commerce in Korea, November 2003, pp. 232–235.

Clifford, Mark L., and Pete Engardio. *Meltdown: Asia's Boom, Bust, and Beyond.* Paramus, N.J.: Prentice Hall, 2000, pp. 216–219.

Kirk, Don. "Charges Rallied Critics of the President: Seoul 'Vendetta' Case Ends with Acquittals." *New York Times*, August 21, 1999.

Rhodes, William. "A Trade Deal with Seoul Should Be a Priority for Washington." *Financial Times*, January 9, 2006.

Yeonhee, Kim, and Doug Palmer. "US and South Korea welcome long-awaited trade deal." December 4, 2010. http://www.reuters.com/article/idUSTRE6B25GJ20101204.

DEFY INTIMIDATION— STAND UP FOR WHAT'S RIGHT

*Facing Down Robert Mugabe,
the Threat of Argentine Nationalization,
and Insisting on Collective Action Clauses*

One of the greatest lessons I have learned over the years is that it takes courage to stand up for what's right. For that reason, I don't back down in the face of intimidation or adversity.

When I was moderating a panel in South Africa in 1994, I refused to cede ground to Robert Mugabe, the president of Zimbabwe. When I was faced with a volatile economy minister who threatened to nationalize Citibank's operations in Argentina if we did not make unwarranted negotiating concessions in restructuring the country's debt, I defied this threat. It turned out to be a bluff. And in 2001, as Argentina was about to default on its debt, the Bush administration floated the idea that perhaps countries should be allowed to declare a type of Chapter 11 bankruptcy. I thought this was a bad idea, and I stood up for the alternative—the inclusion of collective action clauses in loans that allow lenders and borrowers to take specific actions in the event of nonpayment. I mobilized the opinion of the international banking community around the issue, thereby heading off proposals for sovereign "bankruptcy," which could have cut the flow of funding to much of the developing world.

When something is right, you have to stand up for it. Recognize when someone is either trying to intimidate you or making idle threats as a negotiating position. Hold your ground and defy intimidation. For longer-term efforts that require the support of others, employ public means—such as writing op-ed pieces, giving press and TV interviews, and making speeches—to make your views widely known and to catalyze support.

ROBERT MUGABE

Shortly after the election of Nelson Mandela as president of South Africa, the leaders of southern Africa gathered at the World Economic Forum (WEF) meeting in Cape Town, South Africa, in June 1994. The meeting was titled "On the Threshold of a New Era." I was given the job of moderating the lineup of presidential speakers and keeping them to their allotted time frame. Robert Mugabe, the often long-winded president of Zimbabwe, was speaking on the panel. Joaquim Chissano, the president of Mozambique, was there. The freshly elected President Mandela was there, too, and was due to speak after several other African presidents had finished.

But Mugabe was going on and on. If he kept it up, nobody else would have any chance to speak at all. I passed him three notes saying that he was running out of time, and then that he was over time. But he still wouldn't stop.

I finally interrupted him. "Mr. President, unfortunately there are four other speakers here," I said. "You are over time, and we still have to hear from our host, President Mandela."

"Your last name is Rhodes, correct?" he asked.

"Yes, Mr. President," I replied.

"Are you related to John Cecil Rhodes?" he demanded, glaring with intimidation.

That Rhodes, of course, was an instrumental figure in southern Africa's history: a legendary British colonialist and promoter of the Anglo-Saxon race who founded the state of Rhodesia (named after himself), which later became the present-day Zimbabwe, and also started the diamond-mining company De Beers. Rhodes was also the man who funded generations of Rhodes scholars at Oxford University, but clearly the Zimbabwean president had no such favorable reference in mind.

The optimistic mood of the final milestone of postcolonial Africa, as embodied by President Mandela there on the stage, was suddenly dampened by the rage of history. Mugabe, who in his early years had been widely hailed as the symbol of Africa's new leadership and its great independence hero, was finding himself eclipsed by Mandela and the admiring hopes that accompanied his election. Previously the star of the region, Mugabe found himself sharing the same stage with the newer, brighter star who was being lauded as an even more forward-looking embodiment of

Africa's new homegrown leadership. It seemed clear that Mugabe wanted to reassert his importance. He swelled as if I were carrying the baton of white racism and colonial exploitation and he were prepared to do battle.

"As far as I am aware, Mr. President, I am not related to John Cecil Rhodes," I replied calmly, refusing to be riled. "And your time is now up."

Mugabe then backed down and ceded the floor to the next speaker, the president of Mozambique.

Later Mugabe and I sat at the same table at one of the forum's events. "I see you have a strong character," he said to me, now taking a tone of mutual respect. "You can hold your own."

The story of this encounter became well known in African circles, and I became the man who had succeeded in cutting off Mugabe. The following year, I received a phone call from Ron Brown, the charismatic, dynamic U.S. secretary of commerce. He was calling to ask me to chair a panel at a lunch at the Plaza Hotel. A number of southern African heads of state were coming to New York for the fiftieth anniversary of the United Nations in 1995. "I heard what you did at the World Economic Forum in Cape Town," he said. "You can control these guys." Mercifully, Mugabe did not come for lunch.

A meaningful next step in Citibank's history emerged from that 1994 trip to Cape Town, however: I became convinced that it was the right time for the bank to return to South Africa. We had shuttered our operations there in 1987 as part of the world's action began to boycott the country over its policies of apartheid. At the World Economic Forum, I co-chaired a panel on privatization and economic reform with Trevor Manuel. He had been the economic spokesman for Mandela's party, the African National Congress (ANC), and also a labor rights advocate and proponent of socialist policies. Mandela had just appointed him minister of trade and industry a little more than two weeks before the conference.

During the panel discussion, I gave examples of the benefits of privatization in Eastern and Central Europe, Latin America, and Asia, and urged the importance of economic openness for economic growth. "The political change and the lifting of sanctions will allow South Africa to act as a motor for southern Africa and Africa as a whole," I said.

I spoke of Poland and its economic reforms, and mentioned the Czech Republic and Hungary, where socialist policies remained but market-oriented forces were taking hold. I said that privatization makes an economy more efficient, and that it was critically important for a country's economic authorities to pursue promarket policies. "In China, market reforms are lifting the standards of 20 percent of the world's population," I had said in a similar speech to African leaders at the WEF meeting in Davos, Switzerland, earlier that year.

"Likewise in the former Soviet Union, reformers struggle to break free of old habits and chart a new path to growth and prosperity," I said. "Finally in Latin America, an area of the world I know well, dedicated leaders in many countries have been implementing structural reforms and opening their markets to the free movement of money and goods. They are now attracting the kind of trade and investment flows that they had long hoped for."

After interacting at the Cape Town forum with Mandela, his deputy president, Thabo Mbeki (who would succeed

Mandela as president), and Manuel (who would later become South Africa's finance minister for 13 years, serving two subsequent presidents as well), I was impressed. While the ANC had advocated socialism in its election campaign, these men seemed open-minded about change. During his plenary address to the forum, President Mandela had spoken to the assembled group about "social justice," "income redistribution," and "building a people-centered and caring society." Yet in our interactions, he also expressed interest in economic reforms that would attract foreign investment to a country that had been cut off from the world during the apartheid era, which ended under President F. W. de Klerk.

I could see Mandela's great leadership in the way that he handled himself and dealt with other people. He was a socialist at heart, but he was open, as were the people around him, like Mbeki and Manuel. While in Cape Town, I also had dinner with Alec Erwin, the trade unionist leader, who was Mandela's deputy minister of finance and later became minister of trade and industry. I was impressed that he seemed both open-minded and serious about how South Africa could start attracting foreign investment to spur economic growth as well.

Back in 1985, under the worst years of the apartheid regime, Gerhardus Petrus Christiaan de Kock, the head of the central bank, the South African Reserve Bank, had come to see me in New York on the advice of the International Monetary Fund. His father had been the central banker of South Africa for almost 20 years under the British Commonwealth, and the son had risen through the bank's ranks to inherit the mantle. There had been a run on South Africa's currency, the rand, and its value had fallen from near parity with the dollar to R2.40. South Africa needed to reschedule its debt. I told him that it would be difficult for me to do anything to help: Citibank was considering closing its operations in South Africa (though the move would take two more years), and the country would continue to have difficultly with the international banking community as long as it maintained apartheid. There was little I could do unless the government ended apartheid.

Almost a decade later, South Africa's economy had enormous potential, with its rich natural resources, a large population, and upbeat forecasts about the economic benefits of the multiracial society that Mandela had pledged to create. The country had just achieved two consecutive quarters of GDP growth after years of retrenchment. Optimism was high, and Mandela himself compared the country's potential to that of the "Asian Tigers," such as South Korea and Taiwan. I believed that emerging markets were the future, and South Africa under Nelson Mandela's leadership was clearly going to be one of them. He would bring financial stability, oversee the return of multinational corporations to South Africa, and ensure the growth of a dynamic economy.

When I returned to New York, I spoke with my senior management colleagues about reopening in Johannesburg, and enlisted the support of John Reed as well as members of our board, including our lead director, Frank Thomas. He was an influential African American leader who had spent 17 years as president of the Ford Foundation and had worked hard to abolish apartheid in South Africa. Thomas, in particular, wanted to make a strong show of support for the new Mandela government.

Citibank soon became the first U.S. financial institution to reopen in South Africa, and today it is the largest foreign bank in the country. We put a representative office in place in Johannesburg that same year, 1994, and opened full banking operations in July 1995, immediately after government regulations allowed it. "It is encouraging that there is a commitment to a free-market economy, that the country has now received an investment grade debt rating, thereby improving its access to the capital markets, and that foreign investment is being fostered," I said at the opening ceremony.

On that occasion, the contrast between Mandela's economic openness and the closed, protectionist, and anti-pluralistic policies that Mugabe was pursuing just north of South Africa's border, which would ultimately drive Zimbabwe to financial disaster, could not have been more striking. Standing up to Mugabe and refusing to back down, in defense of Mandela and the other speakers on the panel, had clearly been the right thing to do and had earned me and Citibank the respect of many of the African leaders in attendance.

ARGENTINA: THREAT TO NATIONALIZE

I was walking outside our branch office in Buenos Aires one day in the 1980s, and a woman came up to me. She wanted to find out where the tax payment office was located, but instead she asked: "Can you tell me where I can go to register not to pay income tax?" Massive tax evasion was the mentality of many Argentines at the time, and the Argentine government was suffering for it, in addition to other problems that had befallen it.

In the early twentieth century, Argentina was one of the 10 richest countries in the world, profiting from the fertility of the pampas, which allowed exports of beef, grains, and other agricultural products to grow the economy at 6 to 7 percent in the years between 1860 and 1930. The most Europeanized of Latin American countries, Argentina had the highest levels of education in the region, a huge influx of European immigrants, and a rich intellectual culture.

Citibank had been in Argentina since 1914, when it opened its first branch overseas. Other overseas branches that had been around longer, such as that in China, had been acquired, but this, following an act of Congress permitting U.S. banks to open overseas branches, allowed us to open our very first branch in Buenos Aires. So we had a presence, a long-term commitment, and a desire to do what was right when it came to Argentina and its future stability.

But political crises and bad fiscal and economic management by successive governments meant that by the early 1980s, Argentina was in trouble. And it did not have a good track record for regaining stability: the country had gone through an average of one economics minister per year for the previous 44 years.

One of the main contributors to the crisis was the central bank's policy of tying adjustable loan rates to the value of the U.S. dollar, causing monthly interest payments to rise more than tenfold between early 1981 and mid-1982, as the dollar rose in value and the U.S. prime rate topped 21.5 percent; by the end of 1982, banks were writing off about 5 percent of their loan portfolios monthly, according to the World Bank. At the same time, the price of Saudi crude oil, which was less than $3 a barrel in 1973, had risen to $33 a barrel by 1982.

In 1982, Argentina's economy shrank 12 percent. When the military-led government decided to invade the Falklands (Malvinas) Islands and lost to British forces, it was the last straw. The military surrendered to public outrage and held elections.

The democratically elected administration of President Raúl Alfonsín came to power in late 1983. By then, inflation had hit 434 percent, resulting in a 20 percent fall in industrial output and a ruinous run on banks and the peso. Hyperinflation topped 600 percent by the middle of 1984. External debt amounted to $43 billion, rising to $45 billion by the end of the year, and commercial banks held $26 billion of it. Following the "debt bomb" of 1982, Argentina owed foreign creditors the largest amounts after Mexico and Brazil.

The debt burden was exacerbated by a government act in 1983 that allowed more than 200 Argentine companies to transfer the bulk of their $17 billion in corporate debt to the federal government, turning private debt into public liabilities. Previously, 90 percent of Citibank's loans had been extended to the private sector. These debts then became owed by the state.

As of March 1984, Argentina was in arrears on more than $650 million in interest payments to U.S. banks, seriously threatening the balance sheets of a number of international financial institutions, including our own. It was more than $1 billion behind in repaying its short-term trade credits. The International Monetary Fund was withholding disbursals from a $900 million loan it had approved the previous year because Argentina was unable to keep pace with interest payments. Alfonsín vowed that the debt would not be repaid "with the hunger of our people." Confrontation seemed inevitable.

Back in October of 1982, I had begun chairing the banks' committee to work with the Argentine government in restructuring its foreign debt. Our working group included representatives of five U.S. banks, a Japanese bank, a French bank, a Swiss bank, a German bank, a British bank, and a Canadian bank. Although this was the normal practice for countries with sovereign debt issues, Argentina presented more difficult problems. Because of the Falklands (Malvinas) War, neither the British government nor the British banks were particularly anxious to help out the Argentine government. Lloyds Bank only reluctantly agreed to serve on the committee. Compounding this problem was the friction that existed between the British banks and the other foreign banks because of the delay or refusal by the foreign banks to share payments with British banks.

Under the terms of international syndicated bank loans, the borrower makes payments of principal and interest to a paying agent, which then makes payments to the other members of the syndicate. If there is a shortfall, the payment would normally be allocated proportionally. When the Falklands (Malvinas) War began, Argentina ceased to make payments on its syndicated bank loans to agents, but rather made payments to individual banks, leaving out the British banks, with whose government it was at war. When the British banks requested that other banks share their payments, few banks responded. A similar situation arose with U.S. banks during the Iranian hostage situation in 1980–1981. These issues complicated the functioning of the working committee.

The committee began negotiations with the government of Argentina on extending a $1.1 billion bridge loan,

with disbursements conditional upon Argentina's compli-
ance with an International Monetary Fund program and
the payment of interest due on its foreign currency loans.
In December 1982 we reached agreement, and we continued negotiations on medium-term credit through 1983,
through the election of Alfonsín that fall.

Before he could take office, we decided that, with the
encouragement of the U.S. government, we should convince banks to waive many of the conditions on the disbursement of new money in order to provide the funds
necessary to keep the newly elected government from having its loans classified as "nonperforming." Such a classification would have caused banks to write down the loans
and would have substantially limited or precluded Argentina's access to international financial markets.

Although the economic and financial situation in Argentina was continuing to deteriorate, in part as the result of a general strike by labor unions that paralyzed the
country, the consent of all banks was obtained. On November 30, 1983, we disbursed $500 million to Argentina
at 10 p.m., with the New York Clearing House payments
system (CHIPS) being kept open past its normal 5 p.m.
closing time at the request of the CEOs of Citibank, Morgan Guaranty Trust, and Manufacturers Hanover. At 6:30
that evening, our CEO, Walter Wriston, had come down to
my office and sat at my secretary's desk until we finished
rounding up the final banks and getting the required documentation from the Central Bank of Argentina.

Alfonsín appointed Bernardo Grinspun as minister
of the economy. The son of a clothing retailer, Grinspun
was a Keynesian economist who believed that by stimulat-
ing the economy and spending money, the country would

recover more quickly than it would by imposing IMF-style austerity. He believed that by increasing wages, imposing price freezes, and levying a surcharge on consumer goods to raise tax revenue, enough wealth would be generated to pay the foreign debt—over time.

But many economists, both inside and outside of the country, quickly began to doubt the competence of the Argentine economic team. Grinspun would later come to our meetings with an outline for what he wanted to say written on a napkin. He was known for being an unusually blunt speaker; Argentines called him a man "with no hair on his tongue," meaning that he always spoke his mind. Unfortunately, he often had a tendency to get himself so worked up as a result of the stress he was under that he became emotional and volatile (he would eventually die of a heart attack).

On March 28, 1984, I traveled to Buenos Aires following an Inter-American Development Bank meeting in Uruguay, where I had been unsuccessful in arranging a meeting with Minister Grinspun. He had refused to meet with representatives of international commercial banks after suspending interest payments on foreign debt when he came into office.

I went to Argentina in the hope that something could be worked out with the government to keep the debts from being classified as nonperforming. Such a classification would dramatically affect the first-quarter earnings of every bank involved. When asked about this by the press, Grinspun publicly retorted: "Banks' accounting problems are not the obligation of this government." He did not seem to appreciate that the classification could also affect the willingness of banks to provide Argentina with not only balance of payments financing but also trade and inter-bank financing.

As I arrived in Buenos Aires—it was on a Wednesday—Wriston phoned me to say that he had received a call from Tony Solomon, the president of the Federal Reserve Bank of New York. Solomon told him that the U.S. Treasury was arranging a credit facility for Argentina that included $300 million from the central banks of Mexico, Brazil, Colombia, and Venezuela, which together with $100 million from Argentina's reserves would be used to pay Argentina's interest arrearages. The U.S. Treasury wanted the five U.S. banks that were members of the advisory committee to provide an additional $100 million, which it wanted to distribute by Friday, two days later.

The U.S. Treasury, the Fed, and the IMF wanted a quick fix. Other countries, including Mexico, Uruguay, and Brazil, were still settling down after the huge debt bomb of 1982, and they were worried that a nonresolution would continue to keep Latin America financially unstable. Wriston asked what I thought.

I said that, first, a loan of this nature under these circumstances in only two days would be impossible, even with the full cooperation of all parties. In addition, I was in Argentina, with limited telephone communications, and that would hinder my ability to place phone calls around the world.

Second, all 11 banks on the advisory committee, not just the U.S. banks, should be asked to participate.

"This is not just a U.S. problem," I said. "The entire Working Committee for Argentina should be in on it." These 11 banks were representing the hundreds of banks worldwide that did business with Argentina, not just those with direct loans, but those that had purchased syndicated loans as well.

Third, since Argentina had refused to meet with us for four months, it was unlikely that we could negotiate with it in the space of two days, if we could do it at all. Fourth, unless the loan was secured by cash, it was unlikely that it would ever be repaid, and it would just be added to a long list of defaulted Argentine loan agreements.

Wriston thought my points were valid, and he agreed that without the cash collateral, we should not make the loan.

Following our conversation, I phoned the representatives of the Federal Reserve in Washington and told them what I had agreed to with Wriston. They concurred that all 11 banks would be asked to participate, and that the loan would be for 90 days with an interest rate of $\frac{1}{8}$ of 1 percent over LIBOR (the London Interbank Offered Rate, used as the standard interest rate for international loans).

Later that day, I went to the U.S. Embassy in Buenos Aires to meet David Mulford, who at the time was assistant secretary of the U.S. Treasury for international affairs, to explain Citibank's position and our discussions with the Federal Reserve. Later that same evening, he called to say that the security arrangement that had been agreed to with the Federal Reserve was unacceptable to the U.S. Treasury, and that the loan would have to be unsecured. I reminded him that my boss had said that there would be no deal for Citibank without cash collateral, and that without Citibank, there would be no deal at all.

The following morning, Thursday, March 29, Paul Volcker, the chairman of the Federal Reserve, called to tell me that the U.S. Treasury supported the idea of the loan's being unsecured. I explained Wriston's and my position to him. He said that he would phone me back, which he did, within the hour, to say that our conditions were fine and that Mulford would come to the Citibank branch in Buenos Aires shortly to help finalize the transaction.

It was then my job to find the representatives of the 10 other banks to ask them to participate in the loan on terms that could be explained only over a poor telephone connection from Argentina: to disburse millions of dollars within 24 hours to a borrower that was in default on billions of dollars of loans and that would not even enter into discussions with prospective lenders; to proceed without signed documentation of the loan; and to be willing to make the loan with only the verbal assurance of our lawyers in New York based on the integrity of the New York Fed.

I could only hope that the relationship that I had built with the bank representatives would be enough to convince them to participate, even without sufficient time to seek the approval of their credit committees.

The representatives of nine banks immediately agreed. But the British didn't want to participate at all. Still furious at Argentina over its attempt to invade the Falklands, Margaret Thatcher was in no mood to help the government in Buenos Aires with its debt, despite the fact that the military leadership was gone and there was a democratically elected team in the Casa Rosada (the Argentine equivalent of the White House). It took a call from Mulford to Britain's chancellor of the exchequer to persuade her otherwise.

It was in the nick of time. On March 31, Argentina's debt would have been classified as nonperforming for lack of interest payments, affecting the first-quarter earnings of every bank involved.

It was just a matter of time, however, before more loans would come due. And Argentina still hadn't worked out a bigger, long-term package with the IMF.

Grinspun, under the direction of Alfonsín, with whom he was close, as well as the foreign minister, Dante Caputo, was engaging in a deliberate policy of confrontation with the IMF, which was advising Argentina to impose fiscal austerity measures in order to increase its earnings from grain and meat exports and thereby secure IMF financing. In one legendary confrontation with the IMF, Grinspun is reputed to have shouted: "You want me to drop my pants? I'll drop them." And then he apparently proceeded to do just that.

In June 1984, the 11 banks on the committee agreed to extend the maturity of the March 30 loans to August 14, and made an additional $125 million loan on the condition that Argentina would use it, plus an additional $100 million of its own reserves, to make further interest payments to the banks.

On August 13, two days before those loans were to have come due (on August 15, my birthday), we convened a meeting of Argentina and its creditors at Citibank headquarters in New York. The Argentines wanted to extend the loan yet again, for another 90 days.

We invited Grinspun, who was in New York, to give a presentation on whether economic and fiscal progress was being made. But he refused. Instead he sent his central bank president, Enrique García Vázquez, who had no authority to act on his own and could only repeat Grinspun's request for a rollover. We had no choice but to refuse the rollover and receive an automatic loan repayment as guaranteed by the New York Fed on August 15. The irony is that if Grinspun had just come in to state his case, he might well have gotten what he wanted.

The banks were fed up. There had been one bit of bad news after another coming out of Argentina, and the Argentines seemed to be holding up the meetings on technicalities, trying everyone's patience and claiming that they did not understand.

"The only thing the Argentines understand is the cold steel of resolve," Guy Huntrods, the representative from Lloyds Bank, said. Everyone was speechless.

During the following day's session, Grinspun called in to say that if we did not roll over this loan, he was going to go back to Argentina. The answer was no.

Grinspun called again before departing for Miami, where he was changing planes to go on to Buenos Aires.

This time he spoke to me. The answer was still no. He began shouting into the phone, telling me that if we didn't roll over the loan, he was going to nationalize the foreign banks, starting with Citibank. He said that the others—including Chase, Lloyds, and Bank of Boston—would be next.

He said that he would go to the Argentine president and to Congress and get them to issue a nationalization decree, and that he was planning to call a press conference as soon as he reached Argentina to make the announcement.

"Do what you have to do," I told him. I went back into the room and informed the committee that negotiations were off. I was not going to back down, even when Argentina's ambassador to the United States phoned me to confirm that Grinspun's threat to nationalize was serious.

Wriston was on vacation and just about to retire; he had already handed the reins to John Reed. I remember phoning Reed that day, one of his first on the job even before the transition was official. Reed had grown up in Argentina, where his father had managed meat plants for Armour & Co. He had worked as an intern for the Bank of Boston in Buenos Aires. Not only did he speak Spanish with an Argentine accent, but he knew the Argentine mentality.

I recounted the conversation with Grinspun and said that I had told the Argentine that I wasn't going to be intimidated. I just wanted to advise Reed of my decision. But Reed was concerned that the Argentines might go ahead and do it. "I hope you know what you're doing," he said with his usual calm detachment. "But you have my backing."

Huntrods from Lloyds also had to phone his chief executive. He said that I had decided not to give in, and that he was fully supporting the decision. That meant that Lloyds could be nationalized as well. Still, Lloyds stood by my position.

Payment out of the Argentine account at the New York Fed was automatic; Argentina's creditors got their money back. Threatening nationalization was really the only leverage that Grinspun had, and he had no choice but to back down in the face of our challenge, which was supported by the full committee.

Late in the evening of August 14, the committee and I prepared a press release saying that Argentina had repaid the bank loans under the March 30 agreement in accordance with their terms, and that we looked forward to working with Argentina on a new financing plan. We deliberately omitted any mention of Grinspun's threat to nationalize, because doing so would only embarrass Grinspun, and, worse, it might provoke him to try to proceed with the nationalization. Obviously, if Argentina took steps to nationalize foreign banks, there would be plenty more press releases. Nationalization was never mentioned again.

In the fall of 1984, representatives from the Argentine government began meeting with the advisory committee, which resulted in a December 1984 agreement for extensive new financing and refinancing. It included a $3.7 billion term credit facility, a $500 million trade credit and deposit facility, a standby money market facility, a trade credit maintenance facility, and agreements for refinancing the principal installments schedule for Argentina's debt through 1985.

Unfortunately, by the end of 1984, Grinspun's economic program was running out of steam. The inflation rate was 32 percent per month. The service and manufacturing sectors remained in recession. The IMF was losing patience with Grinspun's Keynesian policies. It issued a few warnings, which went unheeded in Buenos Aires. In January it annulled an agreement to provide $1.4 billion in standby credit and $200 million in compensatory financing because of Argentina's lack of progress on austerity goals.

By May 1985, both the IMF and the international banks had suspended new loans and demanded a firm schedule for debt repayments. Grinspun resigned; he felt he had given his all for his country.

In June 1985, Juan Sourrouille, Argentina's new minister of the economy, created a plan that would reissue the peso (renamed the austral) as a new currency. Argentina earned itself a reprieve. Inflation fell from 30 percent per month to just 3 percent by August, and the budget deficit went from being nearly 12 percent of the economy to just 2.2 percent in the fourth quarter of that year.

The confidence of international banks was partially restored to the extent that we were able to restructure Argentina's debt yet again. Argentina never again threatened nationalization as a negotiating tactic. Standing up to what was clearly either a bluff or a last-minute act of desperation had been the right thing to do.

COLLECTIVE ACTION CLAUSES

Our former CEO, Walter Wriston, once famously wrote that countries don't go broke, as any country, however badly off it may be, will "own" more than it "owes."

Inevitably, the joke in financial circles became: "Countries don't go broke, just the banks that lend to them."

Nearly two decades had passed since the volatile negotiations with Argentina and Bernardo Grinspun during the Latin American debt crisis of 1982–1984 (discussed in the previous section).

Yet Argentina's economic woes had continued into the new millennium. In the fall of 2001, after suffering yet another multiyear recession and successive collapses of government, Argentina was on the brink of defaulting on its foreign debt (see Lesson 6).

An idea that had been making the rounds in academic circles for decades started gaining momentum. It was to set up an international bankruptcy procedure for economically troubled countries. The idea was an extension of a commonly accepted economic concept: companies and individuals can declare Chapter 11 bankruptcy protection from their creditors when they don't have enough money to pay their bills. They are given breathing room to get their finances in order, and in many cases they continue operating normally.

The rationale behind the origin of these bankruptcy laws is that it is more economically efficient to allow a troubled company to continue operations, cancel some of its debts, and reorganize itself in a way that can bring a return to profitability. Jobs will be saved; valuable brands and going concerns will continue. This was the case with companies like United Airlines, Delta Air Lines, and even Pacific Gas and Electric while on Chapter 11 protection. They continued to perform services that were deemed to be in the public interest. And then there's General Motors, but we won't get into that here. In short, Chapter 11 has proved to be a productive and efficient tool that keeps economies and the mechanisms of the private sector operating in times of crisis.

So why not let countries declare bankruptcy?

This was a pressing question for the new Bush administration, which came into office in early 2001. Bush and his top advisors disapproved of what they viewed as the handout legacy of the Clinton era, which, in their minds, had doled out bailouts to indebted, crisis-saddled countries such as Mexico and Argentina to keep their economies going.

The Bush administration, particularly Treasury Secretary Paul O'Neill, had struggled with the idea of allowing the International Monetary Fund to bail out troubled Turkey, which was in crisis just as he took office. O'Neill relented after I proposed the face-saving move of allowing the country to put in place "prior actions" before an IMF package could go ahead (see Lesson 8).

But the ongoing crisis in Argentina was another story, and Washington was fed up. O'Neill used to tell me all the time: "I'm a practical guy. I'm not a Wall Street guy. I come from the corporate world." The Argentines are not acting like responsible citizens, he would say. Let's let them go into a kind of Chapter 11. Then the market will sort itself out, and the Argentines will have to get their house in order and get their economy functioning themselves, without counting on the international community to bail them out time after time. It was the old "moral hazard" argument. If countries knew that they had a safety net of bailouts again and again, they wouldn't have any incentive to get their acts together.

The idea of a Chapter 11 for sovereign countries also included imposing a kind of collective loss sharing, forcing financial institutions to also share in the losses. Banks had been accused of lending recklessly to Latin America and mounting up the debts that had led to the crisis and the cycle of indebtedness in the first place. In the view of the Bush administration, both the countries' bad fiscal management and financial institutions' profligate lending had led to repeated Latin American debt crises. They both should take the responsibility for ending the cycle, rather than the U.S. taxpayers, who essentially were assuming the costs of these foreign bailouts through their tax dollars.

The idea of sovereign bankruptcy gained currency on September 20, 2001, when O'Neill went public with the administration's wishes to move forward on the issue. "As recently as Monday morning I had breakfast with Horst Köhler [the managing director] of the IMF and said to him: 'I think now is the time that we need to take the action that's been talked about for years that's never been done. We need an agreement on international bankruptcy law so that we can work with governments that in effect need to go through a Chapter 11 reorganization instead of socializing the costs of bad decisions.'"

The announcement was followed up by a commitment from the IMF to also move forward with the idea. Anne Krueger, formerly the World Bank's chief economist and senior fellow at the conservative Hoover Institution, had been brought in as Köhler's deputy at the IMF with the backing of the Bush administration. The administration wanted to replace Clinton-era appointee Stanley Fischer, whom they viewed as being the chief enabler of loans to Mexico and Argentina, along with Treasury Secretary Larry Summers. The new IMF deputy was given the task of developing a game plan for a sovereign Chapter 11.

On November 16, 2001—two weeks after Argentina implemented a failed bond-swap measure that the market interpreted as a default on $144 billion worth of foreign debt—Krueger gave a speech in which she proposed creating a bankruptcy mechanism for sovereign countries. Under the plan, the IMF would have the power to decide when a country would declare bankruptcy, wipe out its debt obligations, and begin restructuring. It would decide how much a country would then owe its creditors and how much of a hit the lending banks would have to take.

Confusingly, the IMF called its plan the Sovereign Debt Restructuring Mechanism, or SDRM for short. It really had little to do with the real process of debt restructuring that my colleagues and I in the banking community had been carrying on bilaterally for decades—a process of direct negotiations with a country to work out how and when it could pay its debts. This new proposal would give the IMF enormous power. Unfortunately, a few European governments started endorsing the idea as well.

But within the U.S. Treasury itself, there was opposition. Despite O'Neill's public support and his behind-the-scenes encouragement of Krueger, the economists within the Treasury recognized the lack of feasibility of such a plan. John Taylor, the undersecretary of the Treasury, wrote in his memoirs that he sent a memo to his boss, O'Neill, on March 14, 2002, advocating a contract-based approach to sovereign bankruptcy instead.

Under this alternative idea, new clauses—called collective action clauses—would be added to new sovereign bond offerings. These clauses would provide in advance for how the debt would be worked out if it so happened that the country could not pay it. Rather than wait for failure and react, this idea would preemptively provide for a negotiated solution as part of the debt issuance in the first place.

The idea did not originate with Taylor. It had come from a number of economists in academia who had advocated such a solution, particularly Barry Eichengreen of the University of California at Berkeley, as well as governments in emerging market countries. Within the U.S. Treasury, there was support for adding the clauses to contracts, but it would require the cooperation of the countries that wanted to issue bonds and of the investment bankers and lawyers involved in structuring the deals.

That's when I entered the debate. On March 22, I wrote an op-ed piece in the *Financial Times* arguing against the SDRM. The reaction in the business community was widespread support of my position, and it ended up forcing a change in the IMF's position.

I wrote that on its face, the bankruptcy idea was seductive. It would seem to give countries legal recourse to seek protection from creditors while they had a chance to put their economic affairs in order.

But it would take at least several years to set up a functioning structure for such a bankruptcy procedure, if such a thing were even legally feasible at all. No international court existed that could handle such claims. The International Court of Justice at The Hague mainly handled territorial and maritime disputes between countries, not financial ones with the private sector. A bankruptcy mechanism would be far less effective than the kind of direct negotiations we had always used bilaterally to work out a country's debt payments, I wrote.

Countries such as Argentina, Ecuador, and Russia hardly needed the IMF's blessing to declare bankruptcy and a moratorium on payments, as we had seen through their unilateral actions, I argued. And the consequences of allowing a legal declaration of bankruptcy would be uncertainty in the markets, deterrence of potential lenders and investors, and a rise in the borrowing costs for countries in the future.

A formal bankruptcy mechanism would encourage more restructurings, thereby tainting "emerging markets" as a whole and threatening a contagion that could spread widely, I wrote. After all, if one country suddenly decided that it could declare bankruptcy and not pay off the debts that it had been accruing for decades, why wouldn't all of them?

The consequences would be reduced capital flows from the private sector and the need for more government and official-sector loans to fill the deficit—because, after all, the developing world still needed loans to develop. Where would the future funds come from if the private sector was scared off from the process?

In times of a short-term liquidity crisis, as happens in countries from time to time, those countries might succumb to domestic political pressure to file for bankruptcy, worsening market sentiment and delaying their return to growth. Eventual reentry to capital markets could be substantially delayed and more difficult to achieve, I said.

Instead, voluntary rescheduling and restructuring of debts by countries such as Brazil and South Korea, accompanied by domestic economic reforms, had demonstrated that countries that sit down to work out their debts with their creditors on their own can quickly return to market access and economic growth.

In addition, a formal bankruptcy mechanism would create a conflict of interest for the IMF, which itself is a major lender to the developing world. If it had the power to determine who got paid and how much, why would it not put its own interests first? In fact, the IMF already had a history in this regard. The private-sector banks would routinely take debt reductions of 35 to 45 percent during debt restructuring negotiations. But the IMF and the Paris Club of government lenders allowed such reductions only in the case of "highly indebted" countries.

A better idea, I wrote, was adding collective action clauses into contracts from the outset. They should be accompanied by measures aimed at preventing crises in the first place: improved risk-management procedures on the part of lenders, strengthened economic surveillance by the IMF, greater transparency and communication with investors by debtor countries, sensible exchange-rate policies, prudent fiscal policies, and financial-sector reform.

As it turned out, my op-ed piece mobilized the opposition in the financial industry. Taylor, in his book, wrote that it "did begin to catalyze private sector opposition to the IMF's proposal. Partly in reaction to the criticism from people like Rhodes, the IMF began to modify its proposal." It soon became clear that without the support of the private sector, the SDRM bankruptcy idea was doomed.

On April 1, Krueger gave a speech in which she maintained the SDRM idea, but she called for a newly created bankruptcy court instead of the IMF to make the decisions.

Then, on April 2, it seemed clear that the position of the U.S. Treasury was starting to catalyze around the idea of collective action clauses instead. Undersecretary Taylor proposed specifics for the types of clauses that could be employed. Having the undersecretary's speech in favor of another type of solution just one day after the IMF's continued advocacy of the bankruptcy mechanism set off a flurry of stories about Washington infighting and the lack of a cohesive strategy within the Bush administration.

O'Neill then made a double-sided executive decision to quell the unease: push for including collective action clauses now, but also encourage continued work and discussion on the SDRM bankruptcy idea in the future, according to Taylor's memoir.

The two-way approach led to an acrimonious meeting at the U.S. Treasury in Washington on September 26, which I and other members of the private sector as well as the G-7 governments (the United States, Britain, Canada, France, Germany, Italy, and Japan) were invited to attend. I argued for killing the bankruptcy idea outright. The G-7 governments were unwilling to come out against it. Taylor, who hosted the meeting and was officially tasked with supporting both collective action clauses and the SDRM at the same time, was stuck between the two sides. We were at loggerheads.

On December 6, O'Neill resigned from the Treasury and was replaced by John Snow, another private-sector executive, who had been CEO of the railroad company CSX.

About two weeks into his tenure, we had breakfast together. Snow wanted my views on international finance. He asked me about debt restructuring and the idea of pursuing the bankruptcy mechanism for sovereign governments that O'Neill had left behind as the official position of the U.S. government.

I told him that it wasn't practical, that it would put the private sector off lending, and that it would wreck the market for countries that needed to borrow. Not only were the creditors opposed to the idea, but most of the borrowing countries were as well. I expressed my concern that the IMF would be given monopolistic power over private debt renegotiations, even though it had proposed that a separate bankruptcy "panel" be set up. Investors viewed it as dangerous to have the IMF take control of private-sector transactions. I said that I felt this would just screw up the markets. I gave him a copy of my op-ed piece.

I told him that I was working hard to get a country to be the first to issue a bond with collective action clauses. It would be a model for the world to follow.

In January 2003, we had begun working with Mexico to be that first country, as it resisted the idea of declaring bankruptcy, as did its creditors. It was superbly appropriate that Mexico, the country where the debt crisis of Latin America originated in 1982, would deliver a possible solution.

Working with Francisco (Paco) Gil Díaz, Mexico's finance secretary, and his deputy, Agustín Carstens, we came up with a $1 billion 12-year global bond with clauses that would enable 75 percent of creditors to work out a restructuring. Previously, we had worked with the idea of 90 percent of banks going along with a restructuring, the concept of "critical mass" that we had developed during the 1982 crisis (see Lesson 3).

On February 24, Gil Díaz and Carstens met with Snow in Washington and informed him of their plans. Snow told them that if they went ahead with this model of including the first collective action clauses, he would officially drop Washington's support of the SDRM bankruptcy idea and endorse the clauses as the solution instead, according to Taylor's book.

The offering went ahead on February 26. It was over-subscribed, with a spread of 312.5 basis points. That meant that the investing community attached no additional premium for adding the clauses. For the issuing country, there was no additional cost of borrowing. There could not have been a better reception in the market.

With that offering, we started to embed the idea of a 75 percent negotiated solution to debt, with the agreement of 75 percent of creditors. By then, almost all of the world's emerging-market debt was being raised in the capital markets, rather than through direct loans from banks like Citibank.

Uruguay then followed Mexico's lead, replacing all of its $5.3 billion in bonds with new ones with longer maturities and bearing collective action clauses, making them easier to restructure in the event that the country couldn't pay (see Lesson 2).

Support had been growing in the private and public sectors to adopt an approach centered on collective action clauses for sovereign bonds and the establishment of a code of conduct, which later evolved into what is now the Institute of International Finance's "Principles for Stable Capital Flows and Fair Debt Restructuring in Emerging Markets," to guide the behavior of creditors, debtors, and international institutions in helping to prevent and resolve crises.

These changes created a much more dynamic market. By including the new legal clauses, they gave hope to the idea that bad debt could be worked out contractually, rather than through a legal framework for sovereign bankruptcy. They made emerging-market debt more attractive to a wider class of investors, because those investors had a clear game plan for what would happen if the country could not pay.

As a result, most sovereign countries began to include these clauses when issuing debt. They became a template that was quickly adopted around the world: by Chile, Colombia, Costa Rica, Panama, Belize, Guatemala, South Korea, Italy, Peru, Poland, South Africa, and Venezuela. In the future, any outright "defaults" would now have a prenegotiated arrangement.

Incidentally, on August 1, Deputy Finance Minister Carstens became one of the deputy managing directors of the IMF, along with Anne Krueger. He then became Mexico's finance secretary and then head of the Banco de México, the central bank.

By standing up for what was right and fighting off the idea of sovereign bankruptcy, we ended up with a major step toward resolving future sovereign debt crises.

———

BACKING DOWN when you think you are correct is a sign of weakness that others can exploit. That's why it's important to stand up in the face of intimidation. When you believe that something is right, stand up for it. Make sure of your facts. Don't back down, even when you are being bullied or insulted or both. If it's a situation that requires enlisting the support of others, use public means, such as writing op-ed pieces in newspapers and making phone calls to your contacts and friends. Eventually, right will prevail, and you want to make sure you are part of it.

BIBLIOGRAPHY

ROBERT MUGABE

"Address by President of the Republic of South Africa, Nelson Mandela, at the World Economic Forum, Southern Africa Summit," Cape Town, June 9, 1994. http://www.anc.org.za/ ancdocs/ history/Mandela/1994/sp940609.html, accessed June 21, 2009.

"Citibank Opens a Branch in South Africa." *Business Wire,* July 26, 1995.

ARGENTINA

Blustein, Paul. *And the Money Kept Rolling In (and Out): Wall Street, the IMF and the Bankrupting of Argentina.* New York: Public-Affairs, 2005, pp. 16–17.

"Business Notes Argentina." *Time,* March 4, 1985.

DeMott, John S., and Gisela Bolte. "A Plan, at Long Last a Plan." *Time,* October 8, 1984.

———

Gilpin, Kenneth. "Man in the News: Bernardo Grinspun, an Argentine Minister Known for Blunt Talk." *New York Times,* March 29, 1984.

Ginger, Henry, Milt Freudenheim, and Richard Levine. "Argentina Keeps Its Credit Rating." *New York Times,* July 1, 1984.

Lewis, Daniel K. *The History of Argentina.* New York: Palgrave Macmillan, 2003, pp. 152–153.

Ruge-Murcia, Francisco J. "Heterodox Inflation Stabilization in Argentina, Brazil and Israel." Centre de Recherche et Développement en Économique (CRDE) and Département de Sciences Économiques, Université de Montréal, May 1997. https://papyrus.bib.umontreal.ca/jspui/bitstream/1866/444/1/9707.pdf, accessed June 27, 2009.

Schumacher, Edward. "Tackling Argentina's Wayward Economy." *New York Times,* March 4, 1984.

COLLECTIVE ACTION CLAUSES

"IIF Calls for Action to Strengthen the Global Outlook and the International Financial System." IIF press release, April 1, 2003.

Institute of International Finance, Inc. "Principles for Stable Capital Flows and Fair Debt Restructuring in Emerging Markets." March 31, 2005.

Rhodes, William. "Comment & Analysis: The Drawbacks of an Orderly Rescue." *Financial Times,* March 22, 2002, p. 13.

Taylor, John B. *Global Financial Warriors: The Untold Story of International Finance in the Post-9/11 World.* New York: W. W. Norton & Co., 2007, pp. 110–132.

LESSON 6

WEIJI—SEIZE YOUR OPPORTUNITIES

Citibank's Expansion in Eastern Europe, Argentina's Default, and Not Merging with Bank of America

*W*eiji, in Chinese, is the word for "crisis." In fact, it is two words combined into one. *Wei* means "danger," and *ji* means "opportunity." Together, they mean "crisis." *Weiji* can lead to successes—the kind that stem from turning a crisis into an opportunity. But when the opportunities are not seized—or worse, are not even recognized—it is a failure of *weiji*.

Pursuing the opportunity created by the fall of the Berlin Wall in 1989 led to Citibank's opening throughout the countries in the former Soviet sphere of influence—despite the economic downturn in the United States at the time. Our expansion in Eastern Europe was a resounding *weiji* success story. Argentina, however, represented a failure of *weiji*. Faced with mounting arrears, the country chose to default on its loans rather than work with the opportunity handed to it by the international banking community to restructure its debt. *Weiji* failed again when, in 1996, I tried to engineer a merger of Citibank with Bank of America. If that opportunity had been realized, then Citibank might not have joined with Travelers Group two years later, and the course of U.S. banking history might have been different.

These examples demonstrate how a failure to seize an opportunity is sometimes the biggest failure of all—and how new opportunities can come in the midst of a crisis. First and foremost, you must understand the urgency to act. And you must not miss the future because you are preoccupied with the present.

EASTERN EUROPE

When I first visited Poland, on a mission with the Council on Foreign Relations in May 1987, we took a vote as to whom we should see: President Wojciech Jaruzelski or Lech Walesa.

Lech Walesa won. This was before he became president, of course. Poland was still under Communist rule, and as the founder of the outlawed Solidarity free trade union, Walesa effectively headed the opposition to the government in Warsaw. He was restricted to Gdansk, the industrial city that is home to the shipyard where Walesa had organized the massive labor strikes that led to his winning the Nobel Peace Prize in 1983. I had been asked by John C. Whitehead, the deputy secretary of state under President Ronald Reagan, to represent the financial community on the trip.

At the time, the government was led by General Jaruzelski. We were informed that if we wanted to see Walesa, we would not be permitted to meet the senior leadership of the Polish government as well. The whole idea of our trip was to improve the broken relations between Warsaw and Washington. Still, it was an easy vote. We went to Gdansk.

Walesa turned out to be the single most impressive person I had met in Eastern Europe. I left that meeting with the belief that he would one day lead Poland, which he eventually went on to do as its elected president. He was talkative, loud, and larger than life. We had lunch with him in the rectory of St. Bridget's Church—the church where the charismatic anti-Communist priest Jerzy Popieluszko, the pastor of Solidarity, had served before he was assassinated in 1984 by internal intelligence agents for his sermons criticizing the regime. The church had become a symbol in the struggle against Communism.

With the hope engendered by that meeting, it was easy to imagine a new kind of Poland, one without the oppression and austerity of Communism. The butcher shops we passed had just a few links of kielbasa in the windows—no poultry, no meat, no signs of the abundance that I would see on subsequent trips after the fall of Communism. I could envision the political opening that Walesa had started spreading to the economic and financial sectors as well, and Citibank being a part of it.

It would not be long before I had the opportunity. But by the time it came—as Communism was falling and a non-Communist government was elected in Poland—Citibank was reeling from financial problems back home.

As it turned out, getting back to New York was an adventure all its own, and I made a decision that turned out to be the most crucial of my life. The night before we were scheduled to leave, the U.S. Mission held a reception for us. Casually in conversation, the U.S. economic attaché asked me how I was getting home. I said that I had to return immediately because I was in the midst of Latin American debt negotiations, and that I was taking the Pan Am flight to Frankfurt and then on to New York. He said that there was a direct charter flight on LOT Polish Airlines that was bringing a group of Polish Americans to New York from Warsaw, and that if I wanted a seat on it, it would save me the three- or four-hour layover in Frankfurt. I knew that LOT flew Ilyushin planes, which were made in Russia, and that spare parts weren't so easy to come by, given the economic troubles faced by these statist economies. There had been a LOT crash caused by mechanical failure that had killed 87 people just seven years earlier, and the memory was still fresh.

I said no thanks and arrived at the airport for my Pan Am flight the following morning. Coincidentally, the Polish Americans were at the airport at the same hour, buying vodka from the duty-free shop, and our planes left almost simultaneously, at 10:18 a.m.

When I reached Frankfurt I heard the news: the LOT flight had crashed outside of Warsaw, killing all 183 people aboard. The plane had had engine trouble after takeoff because of faulty bearings in the engine that had caused a fire, and it had tried to return to its base. An investigation at the time centered around whether the military authorities refused permission for the plane to make an emergency landing at the nearest airstrip, a Warsaw Pact fighter base in Modlin, about 35 miles north of Warsaw. The plane crashed into a nature reserve on the outskirts of Warsaw, seven miles from the airport runway. Soon after the crash, LOT started ordering Boeing 767s for its transatlantic routes.

My second trip to Poland, in December 1989, was thankfully less tragic. Paul Volcker, who had become an investment advisor in New York after leaving his position as chairman of the Federal Reserve, was leading a group of senior economists, former ministers of finance, and members of the private sector to advise Leszek Balcerowicz, Poland's new finance minister and deputy premier, on the formulation of his now famous "shock" program. The trip was organized by George Soros, the well-known Hungarian-born hedge fund owner, who had fled the Eastern bloc and who was now working through his foundations to promote democratization there.

On the trip were Jacob Frenkel of the IMF (and later Israel's central banker) and Stanley Fischer from the World Bank (also subsequently Israel's central banker), among others—including Onno Ruding, who had just ended his term as minister of finance of the Netherlands. We were housed in the state guesthouse directly in front of the Soviet Embassy, a potent reminder that while the iron curtain had fallen, its economic forces had yet to be cast aside.

Ultimately, Balcerowicz's program not only turned around Poland's economy after the fall of the iron curtain, but it also led the way forward for economic reform throughout other Eastern European former Soviet bloc countries. It was the first comprehensive implementation of market reforms in the former Soviet bloc. Volcker, with a sense of humor, likes to joke that it is not clear whether the program succeeded because Balcerowicz listened to us or because he decided to ignore our advice. Balcerowicz was an economist who had had the rare opportunity to receive an MBA in the United States (at St. John's University in New York) during the 1970s. When he returned to Poland, he joined the Solidarity movement and advised Walesa on economic policy, which resulted in his being forced to leave the Communist Party. His "Balcerowicz plan" was introduced on January 1, 1990.

Balcerowicz succeeded in stabilizing the currency, scrapping price controls, making the zloty convertible, ending hyperinflation, and introducing the first stage of market reforms. He played a vital role in gaining international support for Poland, particularly from the IMF. Most economists agree that without his plan, which was controversial at home because it sacrificed short-term gains for long-term growth, modern Poland would be worse off today. Poland's economic growth between 1989 and 2000 was among the highest of all post-Communist economies.

After hearing the nascent beginnings of his shock therapy plan on our trip, I came back and worked to convince our board that it was time to take the opportunity—both that presented by the crisis in the United States when other companies were retrenching, and that presented by the end of the cold war—to move into Eastern Europe.

The Berlin Wall had fallen, and as the flagship American banking institution, we should be there. We had been operating in Hungary under Communism through a joint venture since 1986, but the population there was small and the potential wasn't nearly as big as that in Poland, which had the largest possibilities for growth of all the Eastern European countries. Its economy was turning around because of the shock therapy. Also, it had an open door toward foreign investors, offering generous tax incentives. We were being offered the opportunity to operate without paying corporate taxes until we had recouped our initial investment, including start-up costs and paid-in capital.

In addition, there was a huge Polish community in the United States, and the potential for both their remittances back home and investments that their business leaders might want to make in the newly emerging Polish economy was enormous.

I also had an affinity for the Poles. My maternal grandparents were from Poland, although I never learned to speak the language, to my regret. My mother did. Walesa used to tease me about not being able to speak Polish. He called me "the American banker with the Polish mother" when we sat next to each other on his first trip to the United States, at a dinner at the Links Club in 1989. Although Poland was still in political and economic transition, I couldn't wait to get Citibank to open there.

But the United States had fallen into a downturn in 1990 that would begin to abate only in 1991, with growing unemployment and slow GDP growth, sparked in part by the savings and loan crisis of 1989. The Gulf War led to a spike in oil prices, and the U.S. government started racking up a large deficit. The economy shrank 3 percent in the final quarter of 1990, followed by another 2 percent in the first quarter of 1991. Citibank was hit by the crash in the commercial real estate market, LBOs, and its position in mortgages (see Lesson 3).

I succeeded in convincing John Reed and the board that although Citibank was reducing expenses through layoffs and expense account reductions, we should also be expanding. While other institutions were cutting back, we needed to seize this opportunity to move forward. We opened a representative office in Warsaw in 1990.

In November 1991, I flew back to Poland to open our branch, and I stopped in Prague to do the same. Before the fall of the iron curtain, Czechoslovakia had been one of the most advanced economies in Europe in terms of its

GDP growth and its education levels, and it had just gone through an opening process known as the "Velvet Revolution." Its level of industrialization was still high, and multinational corporations were starting to invest again. It made sense to open there as well.

———

WE PURSUED CITIBANK'S expansion by opening a representative office in Moscow in October 1992. In January 1994, under the presidency of Boris Yeltsin, Treasury Secretary Lloyd Bentsen, who was in Moscow on a visit with President Bill Clinton, came to cut our ribbon. It was the only time that a sitting secretary of the Treasury attended a Citibank branch opening. He was accompanied by his undersecretary, Larry Summers (who went on to become secretary of the Treasury and then later headed President Barack Obama's National Economic Council). They were making a point to the Russians, demonstrating a show of support for their economy and a sign of goodwill. The head of Russia's central bank, Viktor Gerashchenko, also attended.

Russia's reforms were working sufficiently rapidly that by that year, 20 percent of Russia's industrial workers were employed by private firms outside of the state sector. Privatization was creating nearly 800 medium to large enterprises every month.

My minor at Brown University was in Russian studies. I wrote my thesis on Polish-Russian relations between the two world wars. So the opening in Moscow was a historic event for me, as well as for Citibank—and for the Russian economy. Citibank had first opened in Russia in 1917 during the Russian Revolution, but it was quickly nationalized by the Bolsheviks. "I believe it marks the beginning of an era of rising confidence in Russia's economy and her people," I said on the occasion of the ribbon cutting.

"The banking business, like the old Soviet economy, is fond of five-year plans," I continued. "But if you had told me five years ago that I would be here today, I might not have believed it. Indeed, no one could have foreseen the events of the last five years."

In 1996, we opened a Citibank branch in St. Petersburg as part of this process. In early 1993, I had gone to the city for meetings with government officials about the possibility of opening there. I was invited to dinner at the country dacha of the mayor, Anatoly Sobchak. He was a former law professor at Leningrad University and had not joined the Communist Party until 1988, only to resign two years later. He was one of the most influential men in modern Russian politics, with the likes of Vladimir Putin (the former president and subsequently prime minister) and Anatoly Chubais, the former head of the state-run power monopoly, having worked for him in the mayor's office in St. Petersburg.

As Sobchak met me and my colleagues on the dirt road leading to his dacha on the Gulf of Finland, it was clear that he was no Soviet-style bureaucrat. He had a more open style, more in keeping with an American politician than with a Russian one. In fact, he was the man who had changed the name of the city of Leningrad back to its original St. Petersburg. While there were several foreign banks already in his city, he said he was interested in attracting an American commercial bank as part of his plan to turn the city into an international financial center.

When he started to say why a U.S. bank in St. Petersburg would be a good idea, I interrupted. "I have a feeling you're going to remind me that ever since Peter the

Great built it, St. Petersburg has been Russia's window on the world."

"That may have been true in those days," he said. "But today I'd rather you look at us as a door to the world, not just a window." He wanted his city to become for Russia what Shanghai was becoming for China.

Concurrently, we opened Citibank offices in Romania and Slovakia, followed by Bulgaria.

The economies of Russia and Eastern Europe boomed following those openings in the 1990s, and I was proud that Citibank was helping to facilitate that—taking advantage of the *weiji* for the sake of both those countries and the bank.

ARGENTINA: THE DEFAULT

It often takes forever for things to happen, but when they do, they happen quickly. When things go bad, they go bad overnight. That's what happened to Argentina when it defaulted on its debt in 2001. It could have restructured. It could have taken its financial crisis as an opportunity. Instead, it failed to do so.

Fernando de la Rúa, a career politician, became president of Argentina in December 1999. The country had fallen into a severe recession, with unemployment topping 16 percent. The IMF had provided a bridge loan in exchange for austerity measures, but default on $131 billion worth of foreign debt remained a possibility—and with it fears of an international crisis on the scale of Mexico's Tequila Crisis of 1994.

By early 2001, President de la Rúa's approval ratings had fallen to 18 percent. He named Ricardo López Murphy, a tough economist who was nicknamed "the Bulldog," as minister of the economy. López Murphy proposed a radical fiscal austerity plan to reduce public spending in an attempt to head off the financial crisis that was to come, and he pledged to honor agreements made with the IMF and other lenders. He made these pledges at a meeting of the Inter-American Development Bank in Santiago, which I attended. But President de la Rúa decided not to go along with the plan after speaking with a former finance minister, Domingo Cavallo, who had also attended the meeting. Cavallo had convinced the president that there might be a better way than austerity, and so on an early plane home to Buenos Aires, the Bulldog was fired at 35,000 feet after just eight days on the job.

Cavallo came in as minister of the economy for the second time in late March 2001.

On the way home from the IDB meeting in Chile, I stopped off in Argentina and met with Cavallo. It was the evening of one of his first days in office, and he and a small group of government officials were celebrating the tenth anniversary of the Convertibility plan at a dinner at the InterContinental Hotel. This plan, which was initially considered brilliant when it was instituted in 1991, pegged the peso at 1 = $1. This had wiped out inflation, stabilized the economy, and resulted in an average of 7 percent annual economic growth during those years. But the situation in Argentina was becoming dire. Because of his reputation for previous success, Cavallo had turned from technocrat to politician, and many thought that he would someday become Argentina's president. He was a white knight coming back into office to save the economy once again.

When I met with Cavallo in a side room along with Citibank's lead country official, Carlos Fedrigotti, I said that I was concerned—and international markets were concerned—about Argentina's ability to service its debts and about exchange-rate convertibility, namely his refusal to move the exchange rate. Our meeting lasted about 20 minutes, and then he went back to his dinner.

But Cavallo had a plan. It was developed shortly after he took office, in meetings with David Mulford, a banker who at the time was chairman international of Credit Suisse First Boston. Mulford previously had been undersecretary of the U.S. Treasury and knew Argentina well. Under the plan, announced in June, Argentina would swap $29.48 billion in medium- and short-term debt for higher-yield, longer-term public bonds. The idea was to give Argentina breathing room to bring down inflation and restore investor confidence in the economy and in the exchange-rate regime.

Under the swap, Argentina offered four new securities to foreign investors. Two of them were 7-year notes, one denominated in Argentine pesos and the other in dollars, carrying below-market interest rates for the first 3 years, and then a higher interest rate intended to compensate for the missing 3 years of interest. Two more dollar-denominated bonds, for 17 years and for 30 years, had no interest payments for 5 years, with the interest that was not paid being added to the principal.

Wall Street was on board with the swap: Santander, HSBC, J.P. Morgan, and even Citigroup's own investment banking division, Salomon Smith Barney, participated.

The banks' willingness to get on board convinced Cavallo that a restructuring wasn't necessary—that the bond swap would work. The IMF's then chief economist, Michael

Mussa, warned that the deal would leave Argentina worse off. But Argentina went ahead anyway. "We have defeated those who bet against Argentina," Cavallo said on the occasion. "We have resolved our most urgent needs, and now we're going for the most important thing: growth in the Argentine economy."

Cavallo had achieved considerable success when he was minister of the economy for the first time, under President Carlos Menem back in 1991 to 1994. He had put into place a privatization program, along with reforms of the trade regime, government spending, and revenue collection, and had instituted the famous Convertibility plan (see Lesson 3).

But Argentina then got hit by the spillover effects of Mexico's Tequila Crisis in 1994–1995, and both foreign investment and the credit markets in Latin America stagnated. Argentina's Convertibility plan lured imports by making them cheaper, and they flooded in, causing a trade deficit. Government spending rose again. But abandoning the peg would have been politically difficult.

On October 18, 2001, I attended a meeting of the Capital Markets Consultative Group of the International Monetary Fund (IMF), which had been established by Managing Director Horst Köhler, at the Plaza Athénée hotel in New York. We discussed how the economic situation in Argentina was deteriorating. In addition, we talked about how the September 11 terrorist attacks had changed the world and were also affecting global economies, threatening a global recession.

There was consensus in the room that Argentina had to restructure, and I was asked to phone Cavallo and deliver the message. We were unanimous. Then David Mulford came in late and voiced a note of dissent, still arguing that Argentina could do another voluntary bond exchange. I and a number of others argued back that it was too late to do a voluntary deal, that Argentina had no choice but to restructure immediately.

Still, the banking community was mostly behind the idea that Argentina could have no more swaps. Restructuring was the only option. The consensus was reaffirmed at a dinner that I hosted that same evening in my capacity as vice chairman of the Institute of International Finance (IIF), an association made up of members of the banking community, which was attended by representatives from the Federal Reserve Bank of New York and the U.S. Treasury, as well as by Jacques de Larosière, the former head of the IMF and senior advisor to BNP Paribas. While Terry Checki, who headed international concerns at the New York Fed, agreed that there should be an immediate restructuring, John Taylor, the undersecretary of the Treasury, argued for waiting to see whether Argentina was complying with the IMF agreement. However, the overwhelming consensus was for pushing Argentina for an immediate restructuring.

So I placed the call to Cavallo that night, right after dinner. I told him about the two meetings. I said that there had been a meeting at Citibank headquarters of the IIF and of the IMF's markets advisory group, and that we agreed that we had to get a message to Argentina.

"You've got to restructure now," I told him. I said that international banks were not prepared to do a debt exchange and that he had to undertake an immediate restructuring because, in the meantime, Argentina couldn't service its debt. It was not a matter of months, but a matter of days. It was the strongest and most urgent conversation I had ever had with him.

Cavallo seemed surprised. He said that no one in the financial community had come on as strongly as I had on this subject. But I definitely felt that he needed to hear this message as clearly as possible. Argentina had backed itself into a corner. Cavallo had had a window of opportunity earlier, and he hadn't taken it. He thought the banking system would help. He thought the bond swaps were enough, even though I had warned him that they might not be.

He said that he heard my message loud and clear and that he had to think about it. Yet October was very late—perhaps too late. The political and economic situation of the Argentine government had changed, markets were in a downturn, recession was coming, and attention in the United States just wasn't focused on aiding Argentina.

Unfortunately Cavallo did not realize that time was running out. If he had said after my call, "Organize a committee. Let's get on it immediately," the outcome might have been different. It was evident that the existing situation was not tenable.

Cavallo felt that given his experience under Menem, a bond swap would be sufficient, and confidence would be restored.

On November 2, President de la Rúa announced another bond swap. But this time the announcement was made unilaterally in Buenos Aires, without the participation of Wall Street. Argentina would swap $95 billion worth of government bonds paying 15 percent interest for longer-term securities that would pay less than 7 percent. The lower interest payments would save Argentina $4 billion in 2002. President de la Rúa said that the bond swap was voluntary, but he gave no details as to how it would be achieved.

The market, of course, interpreted it as a default.

Neither the Argentine people nor the international finance community bought the idea. The IMF turned down Argentina's new requests for cash. Confidence had been lost. The result of the downward spiral was a run on the banks, massive capital flight, and rioting in the streets. At least 30 people were reported killed.

So on December 1, Cavallo introduced measures to stop the bank runs. They came to be called the *corralito*, or little fence. They involved freezing bank accounts for 90 days, allowing only small amounts of money to be withdrawn each week, and prohibiting withdrawals from U.S. dollar–denominated accounts unless the account holder agreed to convert the money into pesos. The lack of cash availability worsened the recession and imposed serious hardships on the Argentines, who took to the streets in protest. The restrictions, predictably, had backfired.

Argentina had defaulted on its foreign debt.

De la Rúa resigned in the face of the massive public demonstrations and street riots in December 2001. He was replaced by President Adolfo Rodríguez Saá, who held office for just one week. During those brief yet interminable seven days, from December 23 to 30, 2001, after which he resigned, declaring lack of support from his party, Rodriguez Saá officially suspended payments on the country's $132 billion debt, making official the default that the announcement of the bond swap in November had foreshadowed. Rodriguez Saá also announced the creation of a new currency, the *argentino*—which was backed up not by reserve currency but by government real estate holdings—to remedy the shortage of cash caused by the economic crisis. Then he devalued the peso from 1 = $1 to 1.4 = $1. When the currency was finally floated, it fell to 4 to the U.S. dollar. And all this happened during the Christmas holiday, imposing even greater hardships on the Argentine population. It was quite a disastrous week.

The recession that had begun in 1999 had ended in collapse in late 2001. Eduardo Duhalde came into office in January 2002 and remained until May 2003. His government proceeded to default on most of Argentina's remaining public debt. In a deal announced several years later, investors received 30 cents on the dollar in market value and 33 cents on the dollar in nominal terms in exchange for their defaulted bonds. Debt holders received a GDP-indexed warrant that was nearly worthless when it was issued but that has since increased in value.

If the country had restructured earlier, it probably would have been able to work its way out. Failure to do so led to the fall of the government and two subsequent presidents, until the political system finally stabilized with the election of Néstor Kirchner in May 2003—Argentina's fourth president within three years—followed by the election of his wife, Cristina Fernández de Kirchner, in December 2007.

At the time of my telephone call in October 2001, Cavallo thought he had more time. He needed to begin to restructure the debt immediately. He did not do it.

Unfortunately, this was an instance of failure to act in a timely fashion in order to stave off a pending crisis.

BANK OF AMERICA

The following is a tale of how the course of banking history could have been changed in a significant way. But it didn't happen, and its failure to happen was a lost opportunity.

In late 1996, I was in Argentina on business. Instead of returning directly to New York, I needed to fly to San Francisco to meet with Bank of America. I wanted to go over some credit issues with the bank's chief risk officer. I also wanted to discuss my concerns and get his views about the coming crisis in Asia (see Lesson 2).

At the same time, I wanted to pay a call on Bank of America's chairman and CEO, David Coulter. His office was in the bold brick high-rise at 555 California Street that defines San Francisco's financial district. We both served on the board of the Institute of International Finance (IIF), and we had some business to discuss, including a thought that I had in the back of my mind.

In Coulter's office overlooking San Francisco Bay, I mentioned to him my thought about a possible merger between Citibank and Bank of America.

John Reed had recently tried to engineer a merger with American Express and it had failed. I believed a better and more interesting idea would be a joining of Citibank and Bank of America.

I asked him about his plans for mergers and acquisitions and suggested that we think about a merger.

Coulter seemed receptive. He agreed that it was an interesting idea, and that the two banks together could create a more dynamic financial institution than either bank could on its own.

The merger with Bank of America would have made sense because Citibank was strong on the East Coast, whereas Bank of America was primarily a West Coast institution. Like American Express, Bank of America had strength in the credit card business. In fact, Bank of America had essentially invented credit cards back in 1958: the first, BankAmericard, changed its name to VISA in 1975, and Master Charge (now MasterCard) was formed by another group of California banks in order to compete with it.

In addition to the domestic synergies, we also had complementary businesses. Citi had a strong international presence, but Bank of America had essentially sold off much of the international operations that it had started building in the 1980s, giving it an incentive to merge to regain its presence overseas.

In fact, Citibank and Bank of America had had a merger of sorts once before—during the Great Depression back in 1931. The first Bank of America had been started in New York in 1812, just a few weeks before City Bank of New York, the original name of Citibank.

The first Bank of America had suffered big losses in a recession in the 1920s, mainly in Cuba and South America. It never fully recovered. Then, when the Great Depression hit, it lost 50 percent of its deposits between mid-1930 and late 1931. In that same period, the average bank lost just 12 percent. The loss at National City Bank (which had added the "National" by then) was 8 percent. Bank of America had been acquired in 1928 by a legendary San Francisco banker called A. P. Giannini through his holding company,

Transamerica, which decades later built the shiny pyramid skyscraper in downtown San Francisco.

When National City Bank acquired Bank of America in 1931, Transamerica became the largest shareholder, which entitled Giannini to a spot as a director on the bank's board.

Giannini, who had also separately founded the Bank of Italy in the North Beach section of San Francisco in 1904, had renamed his West Coast bank the Bank of America in 1930 when he acquired a separate Bank of America operating in Los Angeles. Following these two mergers, there emerged one single Bank of America again, based in San Francisco—and a single National City Bank based in New York.

Giannini had built his banking empire by championing banking for those whom he called the "little fellows," the hardworking immigrants who were shut out from the clubby elite banks that served the wealthy and connected. Elite bank branches closed at 3 p.m., but Giannini kept his branches open until 10 p.m. to accommodate the working class. He made loans based on a man's character rather than his existing assets. He famously thrived on crisis. He kept his bank open following the devastating San Francisco earthquake of 1906, operating a makeshift operation on a plank propped over two barrels, and handing out loans to anyone who promised to rebuild the city—every single penny of which, he used to proudly tout, was repaid.

For decades, National City Bank and Bank of America vied to become the leading bank in the United States—and even the world. Both had operations in Shanghai before World War II and the subsequent Communist takeover forced both of us out of China. By 1945, Bank of America had won the title of being the largest private bank in the world. Citibank won it back in 1982. The title was to change hands several times over the ensuing decades.

Giannini served on the board of National City Bank until 1949, when he died of a heart attack at age 79 and was replaced by his son, L. M. Giannini, who was already serving as Bank of America's president.

It seemed to me to be destiny that Bank of America and Citibank would merge again.

I told Coulter that I would mention the idea of a merger to Reed when I got back to New York, and that he should take it up with him directly the next time they saw each other.

In the meantime, Coulter started floating the idea to members of Bank of America's board.

When I returned to New York, I walked into Reed's office. I reminded him that I had been on the West Coast, and I told him that I had heard that Bank of America "was interested in doing something" with us. Reed said he thought a merger could be an interesting possibility for the same reasons that I did.

He said he would see what Coulter had to say about it.

When they next met, Coulter and Reed did speak about the idea. However, this wasn't until February 25, 1998, in Washington, D.C., at the annual meeting of the Business Council, an organization made up of 150 of the nation's leading CEOs.

By then, Bank of America was looking for merger opportunities. Like many big U.S. banks, it was being hit by the Asian financial crisis, which had just begun to wreak havoc on the region. At the end of 1997, Bank of America reported a loss of $218 million in Asia for the year, down from a $224 million profit in 1996, even though its assets in the region had grown 20 percent to $24 billion in the course of the year.

But Citibank was in a strong position, having avoided the worst of the Asian crisis (see Lesson 2) and having also recovered from its troubles of the early 1990s (see Lesson 3). Ironically, the two banks were in the exact same positions that had led to the first merger of their New York institutions in 1931—big losses overseas by Bank of America, compounded by domestic troubles at home, and the relative strength of Citibank by comparison.

Reed left it with Coulter that they needed to look into the idea and talk again. However, after dinner at that same Business Council meeting, Reed and Sandy Weill, the chairman and CEO of Travelers Group, began discussions that led to the merger with Travelers Group, and the creation of the resulting entity, Citigroup.

In his biography, Weill recounts first hearing the idea floated at an off-site meeting of his Travelers senior executives in December 1997. He had seen Reed a few weeks before at a benefit for the Jewish Theological Seminary at the Pierre Hotel in New York, where Reed was being honored, and they seemed to get along well. They had first met while serving together on the board of Arlen Realty in the 1970s. When John was still married to his first wife, the Reeds had invited the Weills to dinner at their home.

After researching the idea and realizing that the market value of the two companies was comparable and that Travelers and Citicorp could merge as equals, Weill had phoned Reed in January. He asked to set up a meeting to discuss something. He didn't say what it was.

They agreed to meet in Reed's room after dinner on the first night of the conference, on February 25. Weill wrote in his memoir that he had read speculation in the press that perhaps the reason that Reed had not completed the merger with American Express was that its then chairman and CEO, Harvey Golub, had pressed too hard for American Express executives to dominate the management after a merger. For that reason, Weill proposed a merger of equals.

"I think we should merge and be partners," Weill recalled telling Reed.

"We'd create a company that instantly would be the industry leader. We'd have scale and diversification on our side and a powerful balance sheet. Our companies' market values are nearly the same and we could do a deal where we each own 50 percent, have an even board split, and share the Chairman and CEO roles."

Reed was silent in thought for a long while, Weill wrote in his memoir. Then Reed told Weill that he had thought Weill was coming to ask him to buy a table at some charity dinner. He wanted to hear more about this merger idea. After 45 minutes of discussion, Reed told Weill that he would respond the following day. And he did—in the affirmative, assigning a deputy to the task of following up with the details of how it could be done. The specifics were hammered out by the end of March.

The next thing Coulter knew, Citi and Travelers had announced their merger.

My idea for a Citi-BofA merger—and Coulter's proposal to Reed—never even had a chance.

Coulter went on to engineer the acquisition of Bank of America by NationsBank in 1998. The merged entity moved its combined headquarters to Charlotte, North Carolina, and retained the Bank of America name. Coulter went to work for JPMorgan Chase, and then for the private equity firm Warburg Pincus.

Later, Reed stated that the Travelers merger was a "mistake." He told the *Financial Times* in 2008, on the 10-year anniversary of the merger: "Stockholders have not benefited, employees certainly have not benefited, and I don't think the customers have benefited."

If he had taken the opportunity to merge Citicorp with Bank of America instead, if he had pursued this particular idea, one can only wonder what the face of international banking and finance would be today.

———

THE POINT HERE is to know when to seize an opportunity and not let it slip away. There can be other concerns, such as recession, that make opportunities seem too dangerous. Yet don't be deterred: the payoff can be great for those with the foresight to see the long-term impact of taking advantage of the now, despite apparent obstacles. Remember that failing to act is the same as acting and failing. Success cannot come without trying.

BIBLIOGRAPHY

EASTERN EUROPE

http://aviation-safety.net/database/record.php?id=19870509-0
http://www.sourcewatch.org/index.php?title=Balcerowicz_Plan

———

ARGENTINA

"Argentina Announces Debt 'Default' Plan." *BBC News*, November 2, 2001. http://news.bbc.co.uk/2/hi/business/1633369.stm, accessed June 27, 2009.

"Argentina: Appointment of Lopez Murphy Welcomed." *BBC News*, March 5, 2001. http://news.bbc.co.uk/2/hi/americas/1203135.stm, accessed June 27, 2009.

"Argentina Default Impact Limited." *BBC News*, December 23, 2001. http://news.bbc.co.uk/2/hi/business/1726265.stm, accessed June 27, 2009.

"Argentina, with Bond Swap, Seeks to Revive Its Economy." *New York Times*, June 5, 2001. http://www.nytimes.com/2001/06/05/business/argentina-with-bond-swap-seeks-to-revive-its-economy.html, accessed June 28, 2009.

Blustein, Paul. *And the Money Kept Rolling In (and Out): Wall Street, the IMF and the Bankrupting of Argentina.* New York: PublicAffairs, 2005.

"Former Argentine Leader Indicted for 2001 Bond Swap." *Merco Press*, September 29, 2006. http://en.mercopress.com/2006/09/29/former-argentine-leader-indicted-for-2001-bond-swap, accessed June 28, 2009.

Fuerbringer, Jonathan. "Argentina Plans Debt Swap in Billions, Delaying Payments." *New York Times*, May 25, 2001. http://www.nytimes.com/2001/05/25/business/argentina-plans-debt-swap-in-billions-delaying-payments.html, accessed June 28, 2009.

Lewis, Daniel K. *The History of Argentina.* New York: Palgrave Macmillan, 2003, pp. 170–174, 181–182.

"Poll Rebuke for Argentine President." *BBC News*, October 21, 2001. http://news.bbc.co.uk/2/hi/americas/1598855.stm, accessed June 27, 2009.

BANK OF AMERICA

"Banking: Retirement for A.P." *Time*, June 13, 1949. http://www .time.com/time/magazine/article/0,9171,800341,00.html, accessed August 21, 2009.

Cleveland, Harold van B., and Thomas F. Huertas. *Citibank, 1812–1970.* Cambridge, Mass.: Harvard University Press, 1985, pp. 169, 399–400.

Guerrera, Francesco. "John Reed Says the Merger That Created Citigroup Was a 'Mistake.'" *Financial Times*, April 4, 2008, p. 13.

Weill, Sandy. *The Real Deal: My Life in Business and Philanthropy.* New York: Hachette Book Group, 2006, pp. 298–302.

KNOW THE CULTURE, HISTORY, CUSTOMS, AND LANGUAGE

Avoiding Nationalization in Venezuela,
The Latin American Debt Crisis,
and Expanding in China

W hen doing business in a foreign country, it is often necessary to know the language, the culture, and the country's history and economic circumstances. Being a Spanish speaker has served me well over the years, and I always advise anyone who is doing business in a country or dealing with its people to get to know them well and, whenever possible, to know the language too.

In Venezuela, when we were faced with the threat of nationalization while I was based there for Citibank, we responded by instituting a localization plan that helped the government see the bank as integral to the country's economy. When the Latin American debt crisis hit in 1982, because I spoke Spanish and knew the region, I was appointed to head the restructuring committees for the countries involved. In China, when I was helping to expand Citibank's presence there over the years, I found that gaining an in-depth knowledge of the country's history and culture, and picking up a few words and phrases of Mandarin, helped enormously in negotiations with the Chinese side.

The lessons here are that even a modicum of knowledge of a country demonstrates respect—and gets results. Don't stay fenced in. Get out and interact with a culture. Get to know the people. Learn the country's basic history and be able to discuss its key figures. Discover the names of the leading local artists, writers, and musicians. Wander the neighborhoods. Eat the food and find some favorite dishes you can learn how to order in the local language. Visit shops and cultural establishments. When it comes to language, invest in learning at least a few key words and phrases. If you can't take the time, at a minimum memorize the most important phrases in any language: hello; thank you; excuse me/I'm sorry; good morning/good evening; good-bye. Remember that a little bit of effort is appreciated and goes a long way.

VENEZUELA

As a Spanish speaker—having learned the language as a member of a cargo ship's crew during my college summers in the 1950s—as a South American history enthusiast, and as someone who always preferred to integrate into a society and culture, to walk among a nation's people rather than stand apart from them, I was able to benefit firsthand from this lesson.

It was this up-close-and-personal knowledge of a culture, and being able to act on it when a crisis hit, that helped me to keep Citibank out of the grip of the nationalization that was sweeping through Venezuela in the early 1970s. The actions I took there when we were faced with this threat could be a blueprint for such situations in other countries.

Venezuela in 1973 was awash in petrodollars. Producing 3.4 million barrels of oil per day, the country at the northern tip of South America had only recently been surpassed in output by Saudi Arabia. And as the originator of OPEC—the Organization of Petroleum Exporting Countries, created under former Venezuelan President Rómulo Betancourt in 1959—Venezuela had oil at the core of its body politic. So in the aftermath of the Yom Kippur War, when the oil-producing Arab countries imposed an oil boycott on the United States in retaliation for supporting Israel, and oil and gas prices quadrupled, Venezuela was the primary beneficiary.

But something was wrong with the picture. While there were large amounts of oil and natural resources within Venezuela, including iron ore as well as petroleum, it always seemed to be foreigners who owned, ran, and profited from them. Over the years, oil exploration concessions had been doled out to international giants such as Creole Oil (then Esso, and now Exxon), Royal Dutch Shell, Gulf, and Richmond Oil (now Chevron).

The oil companies were run by foreigners from the north—Americans, English, and Dutch—who mostly lived in nice houses with imported furniture in fenced-in compounds. They often called the locals, derogatorily, "Indians," and Venezuelans often felt that they were second-class citizens in their own country. The foreigners went to their clubs on weekends, lounged by the pool, sent their children to their own private schools, hired other foreigners from back home to work the oil rigs offshore, and repatriated large amounts of their profits. It was a recipe for resentment, and from there just a short leap to the forces of nationalism that would soon sweep through the country and that remain there today.

In 1958, as a young bank trainee, I was sent to Maracaibo, where I later became a bank officer. It is a lakeside city, Venezuela's second largest, in the west of the country near Colombia. It is one of the world's leading oil-producing centers because of the large crude reserves in the Maracaibo Basin. The year I moved there, nearly half of the country's population of seven million people were illiterate, many of them living in poverty. As a banker, I used to wonder how my work could help better the lives of the Venezuelan people by fostering development and economic growth, and creating new employment. In those days, I liked to walk the streets, and I often ate the food on street corners— chicken, *arepas* (corn bread), *carne a la parilla* (grilled beef)— using my Spanish to talk to the vendors. I immersed myself. Citibank eventually sent me to Caracas, where I married a Venezuelan; my daughter, Elizabeth, was born there.

I spent a total of 13 years in Venezuela, moving to Jamaica for 5 years and then returning to Caracas as country head, where I witnessed the election of President Carlos Andrés Pérez, who was referred to locally as "CAP," in December 1973.

I remember his campaign slogan:

Carlos Andrés
en Setenta y Tres (1973)

Another slogan, portending the nationalization of Venezuela's oil companies, which was to follow two years later, was

El Petróleo es Nuestro (The Oil Is Ours)

Successive governments in Venezuela had long talked of nationalizing Venezuela's natural resources and putting them back into Venezuelan hands, but none before Andrés Pérez had dared to do it. Venezuela at that time had just 20 years of proven reserves, having had no major discoveries since 1958 after giving no new concessions. In the meantime, companies that feared all the talk of nationalization and faced high tariffs on export revenues had invested little in infrastructure and new equipment, resulting in declining capacity. CAP set out an ambitious agenda, seeking to compress economic development achievements that would normally take 20 years into just 5 or 10. "We had to take advantage of this moment given to us, pull Venezuela out of her underdevelopment, and propel her into the twentieth century," he later said in a 1979 interview. "This had to be done—and quickly. We couldn't lose time. We even began without a plan because we had already decided what we were going to do."

After being sworn in on March 12, 1974, he started implementing decrees, resolutions, and draft laws at a rate of two per day in his first 100 days in office. Public opinion polls in April showed that he had the support of 75 percent of the population, and he later was granted "special powers" by Congress and ruled by decree.

He wanted to fight poverty by expanding demand. He placed limits on prices, increased wages by 30 to 50 percent for the lowest-paid workers and asked private companies to raise the salaries of office workers 5 to 25 percent, increased government social services, and hired more government employees, so that spending on personnel had tripled by 1979.

Then he started making more dramatic moves: nationalization. In order to lessen Venezuela's reliance on imported products, he set out to dramatically expand capacity in the country's energy-intensive industries. First on the list were iron ore, steel, and petrochemicals. He nationalized them.

I had heard about one of the draft laws, called *proyectos de leyes*, some months before, when it had been given to me by one of my contacts. It demanded that foreign banks sell 80 percent ownership to local interests and not hold more than 20 percent. Citibank, having opened its branch in 1917, was wholly owned.

But when a number of directors of the Venezuelan-American Chamber of Commerce and I were summoned to a meeting in the office of Carmelo Lauria, the minister of development, I was hardly expecting the events that transpired. Lauria had been a banker himself, the former head of the Bankers Association and the former president of the Banco de Venezuela, the largest local bank in the country. His office was almost big enough to play golf in, and there was a cot in the corner. (All ministers had to have cots. CAP was so demanding of his ministers, with all that work to do putting his development plan into place, that he sometimes expected them to sleep in the office.)

I expected a discussion of how American business could help in the country's newly invigorated development efforts. What I got, however, was a surprise.

Also at the meeting were Fred Eaton, the man from Sears Roebuck, which had become the largest retailer in Venezuela, and Fred Southerland, the head of the local office of accounting firm Peat Marwick. A representative of the Rockefeller family's International Basic Economy Corporation (IBEC), set up in 1956 to promote economic development in Latin America, was also there. Through IBEC, the Rockefellers, of Standard Oil fame, owned the two largest supermarkets in Venezuela: CADA and Todos. And Chase Bank, which the Rockefellers also held shares in, owned a 20 percent stake in the local Banco Mercantil.

When we were all assembled, Minister Lauria began. "We have decided that Venezuelan nationals should control the major businesses in the country," he said in Spanish. "That means many of the companies in this room will need to divest to Venezuelan interests." He was met with stunned silence. Sears and Rockefeller, it was later clarified, would have to sell at least 80 percent of their companies to Venezuelans within three years.

Then he turned to me. "Okay, Rhodes, it's your turn."

He went on to say, *"Hemos pensado mucho en Citibank. Hemos decidido por lo momento de no caparte, pero podemos considerarlo en el futuro."* ("We've thought a lot about Citibank. For the moment, we have decided not to castrate you, but we maintain the right to consider it in the future.")

It was just like Lauria to use the verb *capar,* "to castrate."

I knew then that we had to go on a campaign. We needed to *justificar nuestra presencia en el país*—to justify our presence. We had to prove to the government, the politicians, our clients, and the Venezuelan people that Citi was a useful tool for the country's desired path to development.

Later when I met with our CEO, Walter Wriston, in New York, he was more than concerned. Citi had been nationalized in Cuba in 1959, one of our most profitable foreign operations. We were concerned about growing nationalist sentiment in Latin America in general, and about other countries using Venezuela as an example, leading to a domino effect.

I assured him that I had a plan.

So my team and I hit the streets (we called it *pateando la calle*), traveling to the 23 states of Venezuela and meeting officials, business leaders, and clients to press our case. We had breakfasts, lunches, and dinners every day. We talked about Citi's role as a positive presence, helping with international trade and finance, and as a lender fostering the development of the local economy. We were training local staff members in banking roles, giving them skills that they could use in their Citibank careers or take elsewhere, to other local banks. We were doing the right thing for Venezuela. It was the completely opposite strategy from that pursued by some of the oil companies. Instead of walling ourselves off, we immersed ourselves in the country as deeply as we could.

We increased our lending to the agricultural and export sectors. We even offered to help the government set up Venezuela as a regional financial center. I brought in our head trader from Singapore, which was moving ahead with the same initiative in its region of the world, to meet with senior officials at Venezuela's central bank and within the government about the possibility.

And in a dramatic move, we offered the Corporación Venezolana del Petróleo, the local oil company, what was then a staggering $1.2 billion in financing for the construction of two liquefied natural gas (LNG) plants in eastern Venezuela. That would be about $5.5 billion in today's dollars. The company did not take us up on it, however. By presidential decree in 1975, the oil industry was also to be nationalized. In the end, the foreign oil companies were paid $1 billion to hand over their holdings and leave the country.

Ultimately, Sears stores and Rockefeller's IBEC-owned supermarkets were sold to local interests. Chase gave up its 20 percent stake in Banco Mercantil. The Spanish and French banks partially sold down as well.

But Citibank remained 100 percent wholly owned. It remains so to this day—*Ojalá,* God willing. It was only by embedding the bank into the local economic fabric of Venezuela that this was possible.

LDC DEBT CRISIS

In early September 1982, it had been only a few weeks since Mexico had made its blockbuster announcement that it was unable to pay its debts, detonating what *Time* magazine called on its front cover the "debt bomb" that shook the world and launched the debt crisis. Known by its shorthand acronym LDC, it technically stood for "less-developed countries." But since the crisis had originated in Latin America, the acronym came to refer to Latin America's debt crisis as well.

Participants from the international banking community were gathering in Toronto for the annual meeting of the IMF and the World Bank, held at the Sheraton Centre Toronto Hotel across from City Hall.

As taxis and limousines drove up Queen Street and into the drive of the sheltered Motor Court to deposit the bankers and global finance types who were attending the meeting, the tension among the participants was rising. Those

who had been on vacation in the previous two weeks leading up to this Labor Day weekend conference had perhaps
been monitoring the news from afar. But upon arriving in
Toronto, some of them were having their first opportunity
to interact with their colleagues in the banking and finance
community and understand the magnitude of what was
going on in Latin America.

The wry joke that was making the rounds was that any
efforts to stanch the crisis would just amount to "rearrang-
ing the deck chairs on the *Titanic*." In other words, the
global economy had hit an iceberg and was about to sink,
and there was nothing that any of us could do about it.

Actually, the metaphor wasn't quite apt. Our joke perhaps should have referred to *The Guns of August*, the grip-
ping book by the historian Barbara Tuchman on the
opening salvos of World War I and how quickly the world
changed and would never be the same. This time it wasn't
war that had broken out in August; it was Mexico, coupled
with the first rumblings of economic trouble from Argentina as well. It was the equivalent of a financial Pearl Harbor.

I had been on vacation in mid-August myself, in Quebec City, on the fateful day when I received a phone call
from the office of our CEO, Walter Wriston, summoning
me back to New York for a meeting. Mexico had called its
creditor banks together at the Federal Reserve Bank of
New York on August 19 and 20 to deliver the news that re-
sounded through the banking communities of the world:
the country could not meet its upcoming debt obligations.
Mexico had some $80 billion in outstanding foreign loans,
a third of them from U.S. banks. Mexico asked for a rollover of its debt payments and for the creation of a committee to restructure its outstanding loans.

The debt bomb became an international financial crisis without precedent in modern history up to that time. It resulted in profound changes in the business of international banking. It posed fundamental strategic challenges to thousands of banks worldwide, many of which had ventured into international lending only in the late 1960s and 1970s, and it certainly threatened the survival of many banking institutions, both large and small. In 1982, the world was concerned about what the crisis would do to the international financial system itself. The concern was that the whole financial system was going to become unstable, and the result would be a worldwide depression.

Following Mexico's announcement, one of the first key tasks of the financial community was to set up a committee to restructure Mexico.

The question was, who could do it?

Who among us spoke Spanish?

Who had previously restructured the debt of Latin American countries successfully?

Who had the respect of officials in Mexico City and could offer them advice that they would take?

And who could act as the strong mediator that the banking community needed in this time of crisis?

Wriston, in chatting with his colleagues at the IMF–World Bank meeting, soon had to assert that I had all of those qualifications. I had worked with the Mexicans before, when they had served as advisors to the Nicaraguan government during a debt restructuring that I had negotiated after the Sandinista revolution in 1980. I had served as Citibank's senior corporate officer for Latin America after running our operations in Venezuela and Jamaica, and of course I spoke fluent Spanish.

Immediately after the August 19 summons to the New York Fed, we had gotten down to work. The Mexicans, after consulting with Paul Volcker, the chairman of the U.S. Federal Reserve, had asked that representatives of Citibank and Bank of America co-chair the committee to restructure their debt. Because of my previous experience in rescheduling the debts of Nicaragua and Jamaica, and because I knew the Mexican players, I was asked to co-chair the committee with Bank of America and Swiss Bank. Although Preston Bennett from Bank of America was also an old Latin America hand, I took on the lead role as principal co-chair. Our all-day-well-into-the-night session went on until 1:00 a.m.

I had decided, in deference to the enormity of the situation and the fact that the previous term that had always been used for such committees, "Restructuring Committee," sounded too menacing, that we would call ourselves the Advisory Committee (see Lesson 8). The idea was that we would be advising the country on how to get out of its financial hole, rather than just restructuring its foreign debt. Henceforth, that's what such committees came to be called, and are still called today.

Such committees were generally made up of a dozen or so banks that represented the hundreds of other banks that had made smaller loans or had purchased syndicated loans without making direct loans to a country themselves. In most cases, the business of scrutinizing credit risk was left to the large banks that were making the loans; the small banks participated based on "offering memorandums" sent to them by the major banks. Therefore, the large banks that had been appointed to represent them would be on hand to make restructuring decisions on their behalf as well (see Lesson 4).

The financial community was expecting that Mexico would be able to announce a program with the International Monetary Fund by the time of the Toronto meetings, which were scheduled to begin on Labor Day, Monday, September 6.

But Mexico's outgoing president, José López Portillo, had made a shocking announcement in Mexico City on September 1. He had ordered the nationalization of Mexico's local banks and the imposition of exchange controls, further spooking the markets. This news had rattled the finance world going into the Toronto meetings, and it meant that there would be no IMF stabilization package any time soon.

The following day came to be known as "Black Tuesday." There was panic in the interbank market. International banks were refusing to roll over their lines of credit to Mexican banks. Unless the situation could be stabilized, Mexican banks would be forced to default. All the major bankers involved in the crisis worked the phones from Toronto, trying to persuade banks to maintain their levels of interbank credit. By that evening, we had just barely avoided systemic collapse.

All this turmoil had prompted questions about who was taking charge of the Mexican debt workout efforts. Wilfried Guth, the chairman of Deutsche Bank, challenged Wriston about my leadership.

Guth had been a young captain of artillery during World War II; he had been captured in Stalingrad and sent to a prisoner of war camp in Siberia for seven years. He didn't think Americans were tough—not like the Germans were.

Wriston stood by his guns and explained why I was the man appointed to head the Advisory Committee. It was the Spanish, of course, and the fact that I had lived in Latin America for much of my career. But it was more than that.

"Rhodes is the toughest guy I've ever met," Wriston later told me he had said to Guth. "He can chew nails."

Wriston knew that I had had the experience of leading debt negotiations for Jamaica and Nicaragua (see Lesson 1), and that I hadn't backed down in the face of possible nationalization in Venezuela (see the previous section). He felt that I had the leadership capacity to do it again. When I began the Mexico negotiations, Wriston told me that he was depending on me to keep the global financial system operating. "I have complete confidence in you," he said, "and I'll be there to back you up."

Guth later became a friend, and Deutsche Bank became a major supporter of mine throughout the debt crisis.

Shortly after beginning the work with Mexico, I was asked to take on heading the committee to restructure Argentina's debt as well. On New Year's Eve 1982, we signed a $1.1 billion bridge loan to Argentina, and a financing package a short time later. We wrapped up a $27.5 billion rescheduling package for Mexico in mid-1983.

I had already gone on to chair the debt restructuring committees of Uruguay and Peru, and I would later be asked to take on Brazil (see Lesson 4). In all, I headed a total of five committees to restructure Latin America's debt in the course of just two years. When I was asked to chair Ecuador, I turned it down. I was already working 16-hour days and weekends.

It was exhausting work, but the reward came from knowing that all of the years I had dedicated to learning Spanish, gaining a working knowledge of Portuguese, living in South America, and getting to know the people and the cultures had paid off—and that, very importantly, it had been the right thing to do.

CHINA: EXPANSION

In China, expansion was proving difficult for Citibank. The country had joined the World Trade Organization (WTO) in 2000 and started gradually loosening its restrictions on foreign banking operations. But in order to protect its domestic banks from competition, the Chinese government imposed a limit on how many branches Citi and other foreign banks could open.

Citibank first opened in China on May 15, 1902, as the International Banking Corporation (IBC) in Shanghai. IBC became part of National City Bank (the precursor to Citibank) when the bank acquired it in 1915. From the 1920s to the 1940s, the bank—known as *Hua Qi,* or "Flower Flag" Bank—was one of the major foreign banks in China, with 14 branches in nine cities. And it played a huge role in the bank's global operations, remitting 40 percent of gross earnings from all overseas branches between 1934 and 1938. Because of those earnings, Citibank was able to pay its dividends during the Great Depression, which many banks in the United States and elsewhere were unable to do.

We would have stayed, of course, except that during World War II, Citibank was forced by the Japanese occupation to give up its branches. We returned in 1945, only to have to close in 1949 when Chairman Mao Zedong took power and nationalized the banking system. As soon as we were allowed to return, we went back.

That was in 1983, when Citibank established a small representative office in Shenzhen, the city just over the border from Hong Kong. We followed it with offices in Beijing in 1984 and Shanghai in 1985. I first visited China in 1993 and then returned in 1994 to open the first foreign ATM machines, just outside the Peace Hotel on Shanghai's Bund, when Shanghai and then Beijing were upgraded to commercial and corporate branches. Before the WTO, the government told foreign banks whom we could lend to and in what amounts. Even after China's WTO accession, we were allowed to accept foreign currency deposits from Chinese nationals only as of 2002—becoming the first international bank to do so.

So that was the year that we converted our commercial and corporate branch in Shanghai, on the historic Bund, into our first consumer branch. Subsequently we opened consumer branches in the Chinese capital, Beijing; the southern city of Guangzhou, the capital of Guangdong province (formerly Canton); Tianjin, the trading city on the coast near Beijing; and Chengdu, the capital of Sichuan province, in central China.

The point was to begin serving Chinese consumers and to lend to China's growing and increasingly dynamic corporate sector, which was producing the likes of Legend Computer (now Lenovo) and appliance maker Haier, as well as provide financing for China's booming housing, retail, and services sectors.

To get approval to open the Tianjin branch, I dealt with Dai Xianglong, who was governor of the central bank, the People's Bank of China. Serendipitously, he ended up becoming the mayor of Tianjin while our process of obtaining permission to open there was underway, thereby increasing the role of finance in the city. He officiated with me at the opening of the branch in December 2003.

However, going beyond those major cities and expanding Citibank branches to other secondary cities in China was proceeding slowly.

In part to help speed the process, I have made at least 60 trips to China for discussions with Chinese business leaders, regulators, and government officials since 1993.

Also, over the last 15 years, I have attended numerous influential conferences put on by the Chinese government, including for the last 5 years the National Development Council conference. In the 1990s, I was part of the international advisory council for the office of the mayor of Shanghai, a body founded by senior leaders Jiang Zemin and Zhu Rongji. I have given numerous interviews to CCTV, the largest television network in the world, as well as other members of the Chinese press; I have also done a number of op-ed pieces. All of this increased Citibank's and my own visibility among Chinese decision makers and allowed us further access.

Additionally, being interested in and having an appreciation of Chinese culture and its history has certainly helped. For many years, I have been an avid reader of Chinese history. Demonstrating knowledge of the fine points of China's various dynasties, the burning of the Summer Palace, the Boxer Rebellion, or the Long March never fails to help ease the process of creating a rapport with Chinese officials and clients.

The Chinese are very proud of their "5,000 years of history," a phrase that they often use in conversation and in official statements. They appreciate it when foreigners acknowledge their long history by citing this phrase, which they take as a mark of respect.

One of my most memorable experiences in China was a banquet I was given in honor of the approval to open our branch in Chengdu, one of China's more intriguing cities and the capital of Sichuan province, in the autumn of 2005. I had flown there for the announcement.

The banquet, with dish after delicious Sichuanese dish coming out of the kitchen and being placed on the revolving table centerpiece before us, was hosted by the top officials of the city and the province. This honor was accorded to us because Citibank was the first American financial institution to open in that city as part of China's national policy of promoting the development of its western provinces.

The Sichuanese have their own locally brewed version of grain alcohol, known as *baijiu* in China, made by the Wuliangye brewery. Every time one of the Chinese officials toasted with the word *"Gambei!"* we had to drink. *Gambei* means "bottom's up," which translates into having to finish your drink each time and have it refilled again. It's rude not to. Fortunately, I was able to hold my liquor that evening.

Also on that trip, I visited a little gem of a museum, about 25 miles outside of Chengdu, with a unique collection of Shang Dynasty bronzes that had been excavated nearby. I also visited the Chengdu Panda Breeding and Research Center. I have many happy memories—and the photos to prove them—of holding the baby giant pandas, China's adorable national treasures, which are found natively only in southwest China. I replicated this type of trip in a number of areas of China, from north to south.

In all my meetings with Chinese business leaders, officials, and regulators, I explained the history of Citibank in China and how the flag from those early years hangs in the boardroom at our New York headquarters today (see Lesson 1). I made the point that we were part of China's history. We were not Johnny-come-latelys. We wanted to train the Chinese in banking best practices, bring business to China, and help the country grow. We also made a few important investments in Chinese banks, Guangdong Development Bank (see Lesson 1) and Shanghai Pudong Development Bank, in order to expand in China.

I loved delving into Citibank's internal accounts of our early history in China. Candido E. Osorio, the manager of our first IBC branch in Shanghai, wrote in his memoirs about the poor state of the bank when he arrived to take over its management after a few months of disastrous accounting in 1902:

> The Shanghai Office was situated on the corner of Foochow and Szechuen Roads [today's Fuzhou Lu and Sichuan Lu in the old International Settlement district] in a building converted from a godown [warehouse]. . . . To give an idea of how crudely everything was carried on, not a single book was balanced for months. The first thing I asked was for a general ledger balance; of course it was not produced. Then I began to examine all the books we had. When the general ledger was brought to me, I found it to be a huge book requiring two [men] to carry it.

Osorio handed off to a Mr. Gulland, who arrived in 1907 and served intermittently as manager until 1925.

"Considering the years Mr. Gulland was here, in Shanghai for 15 years, he deserved a glowing space for himself, as he had a most eventful, strenuous and stirring time: he encountered two most dangerous financial crises in the money market, but the manner he got out of these messes was without any loss to the bank," Osorio recounted. "Both the foreign and Chinese bankers hailed his handling of the perilous situation as really masterful. To the Chinese he was looked on as uncanny, how he wriggled out of the net which all were enmeshed in."

I could only imagine this as I took a stroll in Shanghai one day to see the building where those early managers had fought some of the earliest banking battles and wriggled out of the earliest banking crises in China. It is still there.

Our branch manager in the frigid northern Manchurian city of Harbin in the 1930s had a Russian wolfhound and a blonde Russian mistress, according to our Citibank history books. In the evenings, he would take them both out to cabarets or to the popular outdoor skating rink—with the wolfhound serving as protection from the ubiquitous thieves.

In 1919 our branch in Beijing, the first building we actually constructed in China, became the first American-owned, freestanding bank in China. IBC brought in American architects, who were building grandiose classical bank buildings back in the United States, in order to give customers confidence in the solidity of the banking system. With its classical style, steam heat, and modern sanitation, the new IBC bank building in Beijing was considered a model of modernity despite its classical architectural style.

With its four gargantuan Ionic columns giving it a regal splendor that fit in with yet also stood apart from the massive monumentality of Beijing-style architecture, it was called in its day "without doubt the handsomest bank build-ing in north China." China in the 1920s was experiencing increasing political tumult, and the language of the bank's architecture made it clear that Citibank could be a safe, solid, and secure place of refuge for one's money. Replicas of the Beijing branch were also built in Tianjin, Guangzhou, and Hangzhou, and the warehouse in Shanghai was remodeled in the classical style as well. A number of these buildings remain today, including the original branch buildings in Dalian, Shanghai, Beijing, Tianjin, and Wuhan.

Fifteen years ago, when I went to find it, our model Beijing branch was being used as a government passport office, but I'm told that it is now the Police Museum. In the old building in Tianjin, I found a branch of the Agri-cultural Bank of China, its Greek columns out front still serving the same purpose of conveying financial stability. In Shanghai, I found the building still in the same spot, but remodeled so as to be unrecognizable from the bank branch it used to be and from the warehouse it was before that. In Wuhan (formerly Hankow), the building stands as it was built.

In my meetings with Chinese stakeholders, I also found it helpful to learn a few phrases of Mandarin that are cru-cially important. Just the basics, but they're often enough. It's not just a question of being polite; it is an issue of dem-onstrating respect.

Hangzhou, a picturesque city in central China not far from Shanghai, was next on our list for expansion, as was Dalian, in China's far north near the border with North Korea, and Chongqing, China's most populous municipal-ity, in the center of the country.

In early May 2006, the party secretary of the province where Hangzhou was located, Zhejiang, was visiting New York. Zhejiang also surrounds Shanghai, which was administered separately by the central government. The Chinese consulate requested a meeting for Xi Jinping on a Sunday, the only day he was available. Xi, who is now the vice president of China, based in Beijing, was in New York leading a delegation of some 150 businessmen, government officials, and others participants to promote Zhejiang province in the United States.

I suggested tea for him and some members of his delegation, including several members of the Chinese regulatory agencies, at the executive dining room of Citibank headquarters at 399 Park Avenue. Sitting down to our meeting, Xi said that he hoped to attract opportunities and investments in a range of fields, including manufacturing and—we hoped—banking.

I responded that we, at Citibank, were very impressed with Zhejiang province, its rapid growth, its increasing importance, and its bright future. I said that I saw Zhejiang, as one of the leading provinces of China, playing a key role in developing strong ties between the United States and China—which I believe is the most important bilateral relationship in the world for the future. In accordance with my usual practice in such meetings, I noted Citibank's long history in China, our strong confidence in China's continued development, and our commitment to be an active player in the market. I mentioned that we had made a small investment in Shanghai Pudong Development Bank, which was active in Zhejiang province.

Then I went on to say that Citigroup would welcome a presence in Zhejiang on its own. We would like to open a branch in Hangzhou, I said. I noted that I hoped that Party Secretary Xi, Zhejiang officials, and the CBRC (the China Banking Regulatory Commission) would be supportive of our interest and that Citibank would be able to apply for a license in the near future. Xi said he would very much welcome and support Citigroup's opening a branch in Zhejiang, given Citi's long history in China and its worldwide presence.

A few days later, on May 10, we hosted 35 members from the Zhejiang delegation's financial group and took them on a tour of our headquarters. On the tour were also two officials from the local Zhejiang office of the CBRC.

They told us that Xi, after leaving our meeting that Sunday, had promptly relayed the message about Citigroup's interest in opening a branch in Hangzhou to the CBRC office back home and had asked the office to look into this. They indicated that Xi was impressed with our interest in investing in Zhejiang, and that he would support an application when it was submitted. Thereafter, the regulators fortunately agreed that it would be a win-win for all, and our application was approved.

A year later, in July 2007, I flew to Hangzhou to officiate at the opening of the branch.

On numerous other occasions, I met with officials of the People's Bank of China, the CBRC, as well as regional officials in the other cities where we hoped to open new branches. To make things happen, I kept going back again and again for these meetings. And not just in China. For example, I first met Xia Deren, the mayor of Dalian, over lunch at the World Economic Forum in Davos, Switzerland, in early 2007.

We talked about the history of Dalian, how the port city and its sister city of Port Arthur were the main battlefields of the Sino-Japanese war of 1894–1895; how it was colonized by both the Russians and the Japanese; how the Japanese had scored their greatest naval victory of all time there, under Admiral Togo, breaking Russia's naval strength in the region; and how Dalian was one of Citibank's most important branches after we established it in 1923, because of Dalian's role in international trade.

Mayor Xia was surprised. He told me that he was impressed that I had this historical interest and knowledge. Such exchanges about various cities and their role in Chinese history occurred repeatedly during my meetings in China.

Our branch in Dalian opened in January 2008. Approval to open in Chongqing came in July 2009, and in December 2009, I officiated at the grand opening of the Chongqing branch. On the same trip, I was named an Honorary Citizen of Dalian and an economic advisor to the city.

Our publicly reported net income from our wholly owned subsidiary in China rose 95 percent in 2008 to the equivalent of $191 million, at the same time that the entire bank's overall net loss reached $27.68 billion. Once again, just as in the years following the Great Depression in the 1930s, revenues from China were having a positive impact on Citibank's bottom line.

The opening of Chongqing makes for a total of nine cities where Citibank operates branches in China, adding to a network of 28 retail outlets plus rural lending companies in two areas of central Hubei province that opened in 2008. And I believe this expansion will continue.

China remains one of Citibank's highest-priority markets in the world. Knowing the history and the culture contributes to success.

———

THIS IS A POINT that I can hardly emphasize enough: the stereotype of the ugly American or the ugly foreigner doesn't get you very far in international business. Staying fenced in, being unable to speak with people and order the local food, not knowing or having an interest in the history or culture of a country or being able to discuss its famous people—all of these things are recipes for failure. Imagine someone seeking to do business in the United States who couldn't speak English, couldn't order a pizza, and didn't know who George Washington and Abraham Lincoln were. He wouldn't get very far. It's exactly the same for foreigners abroad. Seek to immerse yourself in a country's language, culture, and history. A small amount of research can go far. It's the best way to be successful in negotiations, as well as in life.

BIBLIOGRAPHY

VENEZUELA

Ewell, Judith. *Venezuela: A Century of Change*. Stanford, Calif.: Stanford University Press, 1984, p. 202.
Karl, Terry Lynn. *The Paradox of Plenty: Oil Booms and Petro-States*. Berkeley and Los Angeles: University of California Press, 1997, pp. 123–135.

———

LDC DEBT CRISIS

"IFR's Roll of Honor." *International Financing Review, Review of the Decade 1980–1989.*

Solomon, Steven. *The Confidence Game: How Unelected Central Bankers Are Governing the Changed World Economy.* New York: Simon & Schuster, 1995, pp. 205–217.

CHINA

Starr, Peter. *Citibank: A Century in Asia.* Singapore: Editions Didier Millet, 2002.

Syaru Lin, Shirley. *Citicorp in China: A Colorful, Very Personal History since 1902.* New York: Citicorp, 1989.

BUILD CONSENSUS AND USE INNOVATIVE WAYS TO SOLVE PROBLEMS

Supporting "Prior Actions" for Turkey, Creating Consensus on Committees, and Implementing the Brady Plan

At times, solving an old problem can be as easy as viewing it in a new way. Over the years, I have employed the tactic of coming up with new ideas and innovative ways of looking at problems to resolve impasses. Sometimes it's as simple as tweaking an old idea into a new one, as was the case when Turkey fell into economic hardship in 2001 and needed the help of the Bush administration, which had criticized the previous administration for using what it believed to be "bailout" tactics for troubled countries. The country needed a loan from the International Monetary Fund, and such loans normally come with conditions that have to be implemented as part of the disbursement after the loan has been agreed upon. The Bush administration was reluctant to proceed, so I suggested that emphasis be placed on implementing the conditions first, as "prior actions," or prerequisites to granting the loan. That innovative way of convincing the administration to move ahead allowed Turkey to receive its IMF loan and also carry out needed economic reforms. On another occasion, my team and I, working with other banks, developed new terms for various ways of restructuring loans as part of the implementation of the Brady plan, which contributed to the plan's success and widespread adoption.

But solutions mean nothing if you can't implement them. So time and time again, I have worked to create consensus for carrying them out. One method that I employed when I was head of debt restructuring committees over the years was to make everyone involved a stakeholder in the process of seeking a solution. This requires getting everyone at the negotiating table to voice an opinion. If there's disagreement, get the expressed opinions of all to bring about a final consensus. When you go around the table again and again, those who disagree may start to see things the way the others do and join the group. Holdouts can often be persuaded by the peer pressure of the majority. Consensus building is the key to reaching an agreement that is likely to be carried out by all parties.

TURKEY: "PRIOR ACTIONS"

In early 2001, Turkey was facing its worst downturn since World War II. Foreign investors were concerned about huge scandals in the country's banks and were pulling money and investments out of the country—a total of $6 billion in a 10-day period in November 2000. By 2001, the stock market had fallen by half and credit was frozen, with overnight interbank lending rates at one point reaching an annualized rate of 7,500 percent.

The government fell into political crisis as well, with the president openly criticizing the prime minister's handling of the banking crisis. The *Financial Times* even reported that at a meeting of Turkey's National Security Council, the president threw a copy of the constitution at his prime minister, who stormed out, and one of the other ministers threw the document back at him. The Turkish government had taken over 13 insolvent banks by then and started criminal investigations against their managements.

As a result, confidence in Turkey's economy had dissipated. After selling off what was reported to be almost a quarter of its foreign currency reserves to protect the lira, the government let the currency float in February, causing a 25 percent devaluation against the U.S. dollar in the span of a week. The lira ultimately halved in value at the height of the crisis.

In April, I received a call from Horst Köhler, the managing director of the IMF, to come have lunch with him in Washington, D.C., just the two of us.

Turkey was in deep trouble, he said. It needed an emergency IMF package. In fact, it needed $10 billion. And that was on top of the $10 billion that the IMF had already lent to Turkey by 2000 in a previous failed effort to stabilize its economy.

Being from Germany, which has close ties to Turkey, in part because of the several million Turkish immigrants living in the country at that time, Köhler took a special interest in the country. German corporations, including banks, also had large investments and exposures in Turkey, and still do today.

Köhler asked if I could act as *amicus curiae* with U.S. Treasury Secretary Paul O'Neill. The IMF needed to come in with a loan package to keep Turkey from default and to stabilize its economy, but the newly elected administration of George W. Bush was opposed to any such loans.

Köhler wanted me to convince O'Neill that supporting the IMF plan for Turkey was the right thing to do. Washington's support for IMF decisions was key, because without the approval of one of its primary funders, the IMF was unable to offer loans to troubled countries.

The Bush administration had come into office pledging that the days of the handouts that the Clinton White House had been giving to indebted Latin American countries—Mexico and Argentina in particular—were over. This assurance that the United States would always come to the rescue created a "moral hazard" that fostered reckless behavior, Bush believed. O'Neill was also a follower of this doctrine. This first global economic crisis of the Bush administration would be their test case.

As a result, the newly confirmed O'Neill would not even meet with Köhler. Every time the managing director asked to talk with O'Neill, he told me, he was shunted off to a lower-level official. It was clear that the United States was not interested in supporting an IMF loan to Turkey.

We discussed the recent appointment of Kemal Dervis, a well-respected vice president at the World Bank, who had just returned to his home country to become Turkey's economy minister. Dervis had earned bachelor's and master's degrees in economics from the London School of Economics, and his Ph.D. from Princeton. His career at the World Bank had spanned 22 years. As a young man, he had been a junior economic aide to the man who was now the prime minister, Bülent Ecevit. He planned to go back to Ankara to carry out a series of reforms that would engender the support of the international community and restore confidence in Turkey's economy.

The World Bank had offered to put up some loans as well. But we agreed over lunch that without U.S. support for an IMF bailout package, Dervis's reforms wouldn't get very far. What the country needed was a full-blown gesture of support from Washington and the international financial community.

Dervis, in fact, had flown to Washington to meet with O'Neill within days of being appointed on March 18. The reception he got was chilly. "I can't help you," O'Neill had told him. He said that Turkey should just begin raising capital by privatizing its large, state-owned companies such as Turk Telekom and start bailing itself out. Dervis protested that he was not opposed to privatization, but that selling state assets at the peak of the crisis, when they would fetch their lowest prices, made no sense. He told O'Neill about the stages of the reform program he was planning to implement, but to no avail.

I had expressed my concerns about Turkey to the previous administration in November 2000, to Larry Summers when he was secretary of the Treasury, at a dinner at the Institute of International Education. Summers had asked me which countries I was most concerned about, and I said that Turkey was one of those at the top of my list. He said that he also was concerned about Turkey.

And I had helped Turkey previously, in 1994, when Turkey's first female prime minister, Tansu Ciller, was in office. In January of that year, international credit agencies had downgraded Turkey's debt to below investment grade.

Two of her Central Bank governors had resigned within six months in a dispute over her refusal to issue more public debt to fund a fiscal deficit.

She sat next to me at a breakfast in New York in mid-April sponsored by the Business Council for International Understanding (BCIU), which promotes dialogue between businesses and government. An economist known for her admiration of American culture, she had earned her master's and Ph.D. from universities in New Hampshire and Connecticut and done postdoctoral research at Yale University. I was charmed by her presence. She asked for my help in getting the IMF to move on a package to help stabilize the economy, and for introductions to the World Bank and to Summers at the U.S. Treasury.

In discussions with my fellow global bankers during that period, I assured them that at Citibank we were not pulling our lines of credit out of Turkey. I got other banks to agree to do the same, particularly the German banks, which were the largest lenders to the country.

Prime Minister Ciller had introduced measures in April to decrease government spending, raise taxes, and speed up the privatization of state-run companies. As a result, the IMF began implementing a $740 million IMF standby program in July 1994. I followed up with her several times on her progress, including on one occasion when, on a trip to Istanbul that October, she asked me to tea at her townhouse on the shore of the Bosphorus, the strait that divides Europe from Asia. Unfortunately, she had not been able to fully carry out her reform program.

Now, Turkey needed help again. I phoned O'Neill.

O'Neill reiterated his opposition to any sort of IMF help. He said that we should just pull the plug on these countries, and let them go into bankruptcy and declare Chapter 11 like a corporation seeking credit relief (see Lesson 5). He said that the new administration wasn't interested in perpetuating profligacy among nations of the world that couldn't get their finances in order. It was a waste of U.S. taxpayers' money, he said.

I replied that Dervis was well respected in international financial circles, and that he needed backing to carry out exactly the kinds of reforms that the United States had in mind.

Then I gave O'Neill an idea. I told him that the way for the United States to give its support to faltering economies without throwing taxpayers' money away—which he thought had happened in the cases of Mexico and Argentina—was to link IMF disbursements to specific prior actions.

Of course, IMF loans had always come with targets to reach or contingency clauses—called "conditionality"—giving actions that a country was required to implement over a certain time period as part of receiving disbursements of an agreed-upon loan package. Turkey had had several IMF programs throughout the 1990s, including one that had been approved in late 2000, with targets that the country was unable to fulfill. The IMF programs left the exchange-rate peg in place, which had forced Turkey to decimate its reserves in its failed effort to defend the lira in February.

This time, I suggested, an IMF loan package could be contingent on "up-front actions," measures that Turkey's government would take first, before any IMF agreement would be signed, and before any loan money would reach Ankara. This had been tried to some degree in other countries, but it had gone only so far. This idea took the measures a step further.

O'Neill was looking for a way to differentiate the Bush administration's approach to faltering countries from that of the Clinton administration, which had witnessed one crisis after another in Latin America. This could be a way. At heart he was a pragmatist, and when you put an actual blueprint for how to take action in front of him, it appealed to him.

He said that my idea was an innovative way of looking at the problem and that he would think seriously about adopting that type of approach.

When Dervis met with O'Neill again in mid-April, he found a changed man. O'Neill told Dervis that he had heard a lot of good things about him and about what he was doing to reform Turkey. He said that if Turkey implemented key parts of its program ahead of IMF action, it would get the U.S. support it needed at the IMF table.

The prior actions formula worked for Dervis as well. It allowed him to put in place reforms that the Turkish population could consider as being Turkish in origin, rather than as being imposed upon the country from outside by the IMF. Such outside impositions had led to massive public unrest in other countries of the world, namely in Indonesia and South Korea during the Asian financial crisis of 1997–1998, and in Argentina and Uruguay as well.

Acting outside of IMF parameters before signing any package of agreements with the IMF avoided the implication of foreign interference. Dervis passed a law, for example, to eventually privatize Turk Telekom. Other measures concerned rehabilitating the banking sector, bringing down inflation, and cutting government spending. Further measures aimed to improve public procurement, overhaul the tax system, reform public-sector employment, and consolidate budget institutions.

To a domestic audience, Turkey had a "Turkish program," not an "IMF program." All of this was good for restoring confidence in Turkey's economy as well.

When I met Dervis in my office in New York on April 30, his reforms were underway, and he was optimistic about Washington's support.

Two weeks later, Turkey received approval for a joint IMF–World Bank package of $10 billion. By 2002, the package was increased to $19 billion. Turkey's recovery was rapid. The following year, GDP growth was 9.5 percent. Dervis's reforms put the country's economy on track to grow an average of 7.5 percent per year from 2002 through 2006.

In this case, solving a crisis required a new, innovative way of looking at the problem, and giving a new administration a face-saving way to solve it.

COMMITTEES AND SUBCOMMITTEES

"What are we going to we call ourselves?" someone asked as we began working in a conference room in Citicorp headquarters at 399 Park Avenue. It was a critical question.

In August 1982, Mexico started what would turn out to be a global debt crisis and announced that it could not come up with the money to meet its foreign debt obligations, setting off the "debt bomb" and resulting crisis that consumed Latin American economies and rattled the world (see Lesson 4).

As Mexican officials and a key group of bankers began meeting on August 19–20 to start to work out a solution, I was appointed the principal co-chairman of the committee to restructure Mexico's debt (see Lesson 7).

On the basis of our experiences with earlier restructurings in the 1970s (Nicaragua, Jamaica, Zaire, and Turkey), we commercial banks organized ourselves into committees, with membership based on the size of our exposure and geographic representation. These committees were organized in coordination with each debtor country, and—importantly—they were requested by the debtor countries themselves as a way to work with their creditors. The committee system assembled representatives of 12 to 15 major banks, which, in turn, acted on behalf of 500 to 1,000 other banks. Representation was usually assigned on a regional basis, with, for example, a large Japanese bank representing all the Japanese lenders.

Previously, when I had led the debt restructurings for Nicaragua in 1980 and Jamaica before that, our negotiating committee representing the creditors and member governments was always called the Restructuring Committee.

I didn't like the name. Restructuring Committee sounded too ominous and high-handed. It didn't take into account that we were going to be working closely with Mexico to develop a solution to the crisis, nor did it sound as though we were taking the Mexicans' views into account. The name was important because we were trying to stabilize the situation, not extend the panic any further than it had already spread. Panic, frequently, is all about perception. How the committee was viewed from the outside and by the participants themselves was very important. The case of Mexico was a whole new situation from the debt workouts we had negotiated in the past. I thought we needed to chart a new course. Everything was different now.

At the mention of the question of changing the committee's name, someone else suggested, "How about Creditors Committee?"

"No," I said decisively. "Let's call ourselves the Advisory Committee."

From that moment on, and ever since (except for Argentina, where it was called the Working Committee for reasons that I can't remember, except that we joked that Argentina ended up taking the largest amount of work), the debt restructuring committees representing creditor banks in sovereign debt negotiations have been known as advisory committees. Of course, if the same situation were to occur today, we might have called ourselves the Representational Views of the Concerned Parties Committee or something even more politically correct. But having reflected on the issue before the meeting, I decided that Advisory Committee would suit our purposes just fine.

If greed often drives people apart, fear often drives them together. Mexico in 1982 was an example of the latter. The only thing that can unite banks that are otherwise competitive is the fear that things can go wrong. A crisis in Argentina immediately followed that in Mexico, bringing me into that process as chairman as well, and then also spread to other Latin American countries. Acting cohesively and decisively was important.

We quickly developed an unusual international working arrangement among competing commercial banks, regulators, international financial institutions, creditor countries, and many of the borrowing countries. Rather than exclude the official sector from negotiations, I regularly kept in touch with officials at the International Monetary Fund, the World Bank, the U.S. Treasury, and central banks around the world, including the Federal Reserve, both in Washington and in New York. I wanted to keep creditor governments aware of our progress so that official-sector aid from the IMF and various governments could be coordinated with the private sector.

Another key tactic in getting things done was teamwork. I sought to build a solid team, not just among the committee members and those in the official sector, but with those who were working alongside us and supporting our negotiations. We employed the outside law firm Shearman & Sterling, where I worked with a number of talented lawyers on negotiations over the years, including Bob Dineen, Jeanne Olivier, John Millard, Moby Mudge, and Dick Aldrich, among others. Also important to the team were my colleagues at Citibank, both in New York and in the countries that were affected by the negotiations.

Working as a team, we took key decisions early on. One was to approach the crisis on a case-by-case or country-by-country basis, rather than seek a one-size-fits-all global solution. We decided to continue to use the advisory committee system, which functioned well overall, serving the interests not only of creditor banks, but also of the borrower countries.

As the principal committee chairman, I found that the best approach was to be honest and straightforward. Other bankers said that they trusted me because I distanced myself from Citibank when necessary, and they thought I could be fair.

We tried to ensure flexibility in the process so as to respond to changing circumstances.

To help stem the crisis, we would also endeavor to continue to meet the financing needs of restructuring countries via new lending. That required consensus from the lending banks that were more anxious to see their money repaid than to lend any more "new money" to troubled countries (see Lesson 3).

To get anything done on these committees, it was mandatory that we work on a consensus basis, not by majority vote. There could be no holdouts. Therefore, I felt it was important to make everyone feel that he or she had part ownership of the process and of the outcome.

Thus, I employed a technique that I had started developing in my previous debt negotiations: I went around the room, time after time, and let everyone have his or her say. Sometimes the parties didn't want to say anything, so I would insist that they do it—that they state their positions on whatever issue was on the table—so that they became stakeholders in what was going on.

As the leader of the committee, I always knew where I wanted the consensus to end up. If one of the participants around the table said something that I disagreed with, and that I knew was counterproductive to what we were trying to accomplish, I didn't disagree openly. Instead, I thanked the person and said, "Okay, that's a point that bears thinking about," and moved on. It always impressed the countries and the participants that I went around the room and pushed everyone to speak so that I didn't appear to dominate.

Gradually, the opinions of the others around the table, voiced one by one, would be more persuasive than any opinion that I could have tried to foist upon the room myself. As a result, a consensus emerged that could lead to a lasting agreement. Often the long hours of negotiation over many days, weeks, and months meant that participants were tired. Sometimes, when the parties around the table were about to drop from fatigue and felt that they couldn't take one more minute of the grinding monotony of the final basis point, or whatever the sticking point happened to be, that was the key moment when consensus could be reached.

One of the biggest issues was the coordination problem, which means the challenge of finding and dealing with hundreds of syndicated loans worth billions of dollars packaged and distributed to hundreds of banks in various corners of the globe. When a Latin American government took out billions of dollars' worth of loans, that added up to an enormous and widespread global investor base.

When we began to sort through the Mexico mess, we discovered that the country didn't even have an accurate list of creditors. I assigned my colleague Andrea Bauer to start assembling one.

This was especially important because the task we had been given by the IMF was to come up with new money for Mexico and to get a "critical mass" of a minimum of 80 percent of the banks to agree to participate. When we started, we didn't even know who many of the creditors were. By the end, in March 1983, we got 526 creditor banks, more than 90 percent of the total, to agree to participate in the restructuring. My tactics of pushing all participants in order to reach consensus had worked.

I also came up with the innovation of dividing responsibilities, for example, by creating subcommittees to monitor specific aspects of our negotiations. The economic subcommittee, for instance, looked at the condition of the local economy or cash flow and then reported back to the committee as a whole. We started in Mexico. The one that had the most influence was the economic subcommittee that I created when negotiating Brazil's debt in 1983–1984, which analyzed Brazil's economic conditions and ability to service its debt. I appointed Douglas Smee, the chief economist for the Bank of Montreal, to head it. His committee monitored the progress of IMF disbursements and conditionality programs and measured the country's economic pulse. And then it provided statistics to the participants, who had previously complained of being starved for data in the first phase of negotiations.

The first attempt by another committee to reach consensus in restructuring Brazil's debt and raising new money for the country had failed. I was asked to step in and take over (see Lesson 4). When I began Phase 2 of Brazil's negotiations in June of 1983, it was important to differentiate my style of leadership and what I planned to do from what had gone wrong previously.

At our first meeting, I told the assembled group, battered and fractured after months of infighting, that we were starting anew.

"The problems we had before happened in Phase 1," I began. "This is Phase 2.

"We're going to work together as a team, and we're going to work on a consensus basis," I said. "We're not going to look at or discuss what happened in Phase 1. We're going to move forward."

Previously, the committee's co-chairs had been two men from Citibank and from Morgan Guaranty, both American banks. Representatives of British and European banks felt alienated. One had called it "an American party," in which the U.S. banks put their own interests before those of the group. The smaller U.S. regional banks felt left out as well, complaining that they were being dictated to by the bigger banks in New York. The co-chairs even argued between themselves in front of the group. It was a disaster, and Brazil was starting to miss its targets under its IMF program.

To solve this problem, I supported the appointment of Guy Huntrods of the British bank Lloyds, with whom I had worked on Argentina, as my deputy chairman, along with a new representative from Morgan, Leighton Coleman. It was important to create a cooperative atmosphere and a spirit of shared sacrifice. Adding a non-American to the decision-making process and two new representatives from the chairing banks helped.

Then I appointed the U.S. regional banks, which had previously complained of feeling left out of the process, to a coordinating subcommittee and expanded their number from 18 to 43 to have a more diverse geographic coverage. I asked Manufacturers Hanover, which was well respected among the regional banks because of its correspondent banking network, to keep the regional banks informed of our progress, as I had done in the case of Mexico's restructuring as well. The idea was to improve the flow of information.

The perception that all banks around the world were participating equally in the process was important. When we went around the world on road shows to sell the deal and try to get all the stakeholders to buy into the process, I called upon the various banks in the region we were visiting to urge them to participate. In the Middle East, for example, I asked the Arab Banking Corporation to sit on the dais at an information meeting in Bahrain so that other Arab banks would feel comfortable taking part in the transaction. In Asia, I did the same with the Bank of Tokyo; in Europe, with UBS; and so on.

Using my tactics of building consensus and getting everyone to take a stake in the process, by January 1984 we had raised the $6.5 billion in new money that Brazil needed (see Lesson 4) and signed a deal to restructure $23.5 billion in debt.

Our first major innovation in debt restructuring came in June 1984, when we agreed to what was called a multi-year restructuring agreement (MYRA) with Mexico. It had a clause that allowed conversion of Mexican debt into equity. This was the first appearance of debt-for-equity swaps in modern sovereign lending. It attracted new investors, who added depth and breadth to the developing market-place for Latin American debt. Chile, Argentina, and other countries later used this restructuring instrument in their privatization efforts. Debt-for-equity swaps opened the way for a shift toward greater private-sector participation.

In June 1984, at the annual International Monetary Conference in Philadelphia, attended by the chairmen of the world's largest commercial banks, I was asked to attend in order to represent the bank advisory committees. We met at the ornate Union League Club downtown. What emerged was an agreement that the IMF would institute enhanced surveillance or monitoring as part of the banks' agreement to provide new financing and restructuring of loans over a multiyear period. The IMF would monitor a country's economic performance over periods that were substantially longer than those normally used under the standby or extended funding arrangements that the IMF had set up previously. This information would be made available to the commercial banks for the first time.

It seemed clear that the focus of our work needed to shift from short-term adjustment to long-term growth. The only way for Latin American countries to get out of their crises was to grow out of them. At this point, the U.S. Treasury became more actively involved, marking the beginning of what came to be called the Baker plan, after Treasury Secretary James Baker. The idea was to emphasize growth-oriented structural economic reforms by borrower countries. In exchange, banks would be asked to continue lending new money. Baker also called for the involvement of the World Bank, which previously had left the process to the IMF.

While the Baker plan was later criticized for not raising enough new money, a study in the 1980s estimated that banks disbursed more than $13 billion in new loans over a three-year period. It was short of the $20 billion target set by Baker, but the shortfall was in part due to a failure of some countries to make structural adjustments that were a prerequisite, as well as banks' unwillingness to lend. It was also criticized for not fully resolving the debt problem.

Notwithstanding the plan's successes, restructurings continued, and Latin American countries continued to have problems servicing their debt. A further solution was still needed—which turned out to be the Brady plan, the idea of securing debt with zero coupon U.S. Treasuries, as proposed in 1989 by Nicholas Brady, the next U.S. secretary of the Treasury (see the next section).

In the context of my efforts to gain cooperation and consensus on the subcommittees, the Brady plan made previous conflicts on the committees worse. In the first Brady bonds offered for Mexico, then Venezuela, proposals for debt and debt-service reduction needed to be fleshed out.

They had to be reconciled with the idea of putting up new money. For example, the Mexican package included three options: reducing interest rates, reducing principal, or making new loans (see the next section).

With these options to choose from, divisions among the banks began to arise. Tax and regulatory requirements varied by the banks' countries of origin, and European and Canadian banks charged that the options that were offered favored the U.S. banks. If the U.S. banks chose to put in new money, it would come back to them in the form of service payments on their old loans. European banks argued that the U.S. banks were interested in putting up new money only so that interest payments could be made on their existing loans.

In addition, higher reserve requirements in places such as Canada, France, and Britain—meaning that their governments required banks to maintain a higher percentage of their capital without lending it out—meant that banks were putting themselves in a weaker financial position with regard to contributing new money. But to some degree, European opposition was merely a vocalized resentment of the power of the U.S. banks in the international financial system. Going out with a plan that suggested that banks should agree to lose money made it a hard sell.

One measure that helped resolve the divisions was my insistence that Mexican banks also participate in the process by exchanging their loans for discount or par bonds, but without receiving the U.S. Treasury zero coupon bonds as collateral. These came to be known as "Gurría bonds," after José Angel Gurría, the lead Mexican negotiator, who was given the task of convincing the Mexican banks to participate without collateral. That added collateral to the pool available for non-Mexican banks, and reduced the pressure on the Western and Japanese banks, which had feared that their Brady bonds would not otherwise be completely collateralized. With this additional money, and a decision to let banks cherry-pick the portions of the options that they wanted, I endeavored to make sure that each of the three Mexican options was taken up roughly equally.

Over time, with the innovative new clauses and structures put into place and emerging-market countries' increased reliance on capital markets for raising money rather than on commercial bank loans, the advisory committees gradually diminished in importance.

But that was not without first putting out the global debt fires of the 1980s and using my tactics of consensus building, team building, and innovative solutions to do it.

BRADY BONDS

In February 1989, some of the worst violence in Venezuelan history broke out. Riots exploded in major cities throughout the country, including in Caracas and Maracaibo, where I used to live. Protesters looted stores, smashed windows, and barricaded streets as security forces opened fire. The death toll from the indiscriminate shooting was officially reported to be 276, with thousands wounded.

The violence was the result of price increases that were part of a package of economic reforms imposed by President Carlos Andrés Pérez in order to win a package of loans from the International Monetary Fund, the World Bank, commercial banks, and foreign governments—at a time when Venezuela's foreign debt already totaled

$33 billion. A few months before, I had returned from attending the president's second-term inauguration ceremony, along with U.S. Vice President Dan Quayle and Fidel Castro. Suddenly the country was under martial law. Upon taking office, Andrés Pérez had begun privatizing state companies, raising taxes, and diminishing the role of the state in the economy—all well-intentioned economic reforms. But as a result, petrol prices doubled and public transportation costs rose 30 percent. For many Venezuelans, the pain inflicted in order to secure even more foreign loans was the last straw.

By 1989, most banks realized that the cycle of providing new money and restructuring to Latin American countries that continually found themselves unable to service their debts was no longer feasible. Reforms were needed. If countries did not change their basic structures, open up their economies, and privatize, one stabilization program after another was doomed to failure.

It was clear that the countries were not simply suffering from short-term liquidity problems. Countries often ignored the need to make basic structural economic reforms, including privatizing their state-owned companies, in order to lay the foundation for investment and growth. Brazil, for example, had seven letters of intent with the IMF over a four-year period in the 1980s. What was happening was a vicious cycle. Fundamental economic structural changes were not being made.

A growing impediment to bank lending was the substantial amount of overdue interest owed by some countries. These arrears owed to commercial banks from restructuring countries worldwide totaled nearly $24 billion by 1990, with Brazil and Argentina accounting for more than half of that. Arrearages undermined confidence in a country, not just among banks, but among other potential investors, both local and foreign.

We had tried the Baker plan under the Reagan administration, but debt forgiveness wasn't part of the equation. The Baker plan was running out of steam because it preserved the amount of principal owed and even increased it, as banks were asked to put up new money to service the old debts. Banks essentially kept lending so that countries could keep making their interest payments. The debt burden kept rising. Since the beginning of the debt crisis in 1982, Latin America's total debt had grown almost 30 percent, from $323 billion to $414 billion.

"Debt fatigue" was setting in, and instability in Latin America was spreading. The inflation rate in Brazil, which had just recently ended a yearlong moratorium that it had called on paying its debts, was running at 2,000 percent. Its debt was trading on the secondary market at 29 cents on the dollar—in other words, it was considered to be junk status. It was worse for Argentina: its debt fell to 18 cents on the dollar on the secondary market.

Latin American debts and arrears were growing, and commercial banks were slowing their lending. International institutions and governments—the IMF, the World Bank, and wealthy nations such as Britain and the United States—were having to pick up the slack and lend more money than ever before to compensate for the vacuum. Increasingly, there was a transfer of risk from the private sector to the public sector.

The talk in Washington, and in Latin American countries themselves, started to center around the idea of debt forgiveness, and of forcing the banks that had made all those loans over the past decades to forget about collecting on them and to write off at least part of them instead. The banks had been profligate lenders, the reasoning went, so they should share the pain. There were calls for handing the process over to an international financial institution such as the World Bank or the IMF and unilaterally imposing a forced debt reduction of 50 percent. Obviously, the banking community resolutely opposed such a measure.

When President-elect George H. W. Bush was asked before he took office in 1989 what he thought about the issue, he said that the government should take a look at it and come up with a sophisticated solution. "We've got enormous problems, particularly in our hemisphere, on Third World debt," he said. "I think we've got to find a more versatile answer than simply compelling private institutions to write off the debt."

Bush, in fact, had met with President-elect Carlos Salinas de Gortari of Mexico in late 1988. Salinas said that he wanted the U.S. government to pressure the banks to reduce Mexico's debt load as part of his domestic fiscal policy. Bush "essentially promised that something would be delivered," according to the noted economist Paul Krugman, who wrote about debt forgiveness at the time.

Citibank had taken a big step in May 1987, when our CEO, John Reed, announced that he was debiting $3 billion from earnings and putting it into reserves for the eventuality of writing off bad debts, mostly in Latin America. Then he announced a loss of $2.5 billion for the second quarter. At the time it was the largest loss in banking history. The follow-on effect was startling: Chase Manhattan Bank added $1.6 billion to its reserves, and Bank of America set aside $1.1 billion. Manufacturers Hanover added $1.7 billion. Even Britain's National Westminster Bank added $760 million.

The reserves move prompted José Angel Gurría, Mexico's director general of public credit, to ask that this "discount" be passed on to developing countries.

But that didn't mean that banks had an appetite for debt forgiveness yet. It did mean, however, that raising any more "new money" for indebted countries would be harder and require much stronger guarantees than in the past.

The Bush administration assigned U.S. Treasury Secretary Nicholas Brady, his undersecretary, David Mulford (who had worked on Argentina), and Assistant Secretary Charles Dallara to work out the solution.

Starting in November and through December 1988, the U.S. Treasury invited me to Washington for consultations on how such a plan should be developed. In my meetings with Mulford and Dallara, I said that debt reduction should be voluntary, not mandatory. I said that a mandatory plan would be of doubtful legality and would not induce the participation and cooperation of the international banking community in the way that a voluntary plan would. Also, I argued strongly that there should be a continuing flow of new money to countries that were creditworthy and were implementing appropriate economic reforms. The new money issue did not receive much attention at the time, which the U.S. Treasury later regretted when it realized its importance.

It had always been a tenet of banking that debts must be repaid—after all, seeing to it had been my role at Citibank for almost a decade. Yet it seemed time for the market to acknowledge that the debt had been devalued and that banks had to swallow some losses. Recognizing this was a fundamental shift of gears. I started mentioning in my speeches to bankers' groups around the world that we would have to come up with a new strategy, and that Nick Brady thought that banks were going to have to accept an adjustment in their interest *and* principal repayments (in the past, it was customary for only interest repayments to be adjusted).

At the time, some called it a remarkable turn of events that a banker would acknowledge such a thing. Many people had thought I would be the last to change. But I really saw no alternative. While the interests of the banks had to be protected, of course, the long-term interests of the banking and financial system had to be taken into account.

On March 10, 1989, Secretary Brady announced a plan. He proposed a voluntary debt reduction, or partial forgiveness of debt, by commercial banks. He did not mention the international financial institutions or governments taking a hit, just the banks. This reduction of debt by commercial banks became the focus of the debt strategy in place of new money, although Brady still thought new money flows were necessary.

The idea was that the Brady plan would take the old loans, securitize them, and convert them into bonds that would be freely traded on the market. New zero coupon bonds issued by the Treasury would be collateral for the principal of the new bonds.

The first test case was to be Mexico. It became the first deal in which we converted syndicated loans to bonds in order to securitize the debt, creating an entirely new financial product. The old loans were to convert to bonds, and become freely tradable in the market. This was a key turning point.

It was to be the model for other countries to follow. We started negotiating soon after Brady's announcement, including at several all-night meetings with the CEOs of the banks that were on the Mexico committee. We didn't reach an agreement.

So on Saturday, July 22, 1989, I went to Washington with Reed for another round of meetings at the U.S. Treasury to try to close the deal. The discussions were chaired on the U.S. side by Mulford and the head of the Federal Reserve Bank of New York, Gerald Corrigan. The Mexican side was led by Pedro Aspe, the minister of finance, and Angel Gurría, his deputy. The others in attendance were A. W. Clausen, CEO of Bank of America; Swiss Bank's head negotiator, Tony Spicijaric; and a handful of others, including Terry Checki, who, as usual, was very helpful. At our marathon meetings in a third-floor conference room at the Treasury, we hammered out a solution. The proposal on the table was a 45 percent discount bond—in other words, a debt hit for the banks—and no provisions for new money.

Instead, we worked to include a menu of options and insisted that new money be part of the deal and that Mexican banks participate in this new money option. Flexibility was key. We introduced a longer-term menu of options through the voluntary debt reduction mechanism, including debt-for-equity exchanges, cash buybacks, and interest and principal reduction bonds. Brady joined the meeting for the working out of the final terms.

On Sunday night just before midnight, Clausen, Reed, Spicijaric, and I met with the 15 member banks of the Mexico Advisory Committee representing the 400 or more commercial banks that held Mexican debt at the offices of the Bankers' Association for Foreign Trade, which I had chosen for our meeting place because I had been the organization's president. We announced that a compromise arrangement had been put forward.

The banks could cut the value of their principal by 35 percent (discount bonds); they could reduce interest rates by 35 percent, to 6.25 percent (par bonds); or they could make new loans equal to 25 percent of their existing medium- and long-term loans (new money bonds) to help fund Mexico's continued growth.

The par and discount bonds would be collateralized by U.S. Treasury 30-year zero coupon bonds funded by a multibillion-dollar consortium of funds from the IMF, the World Bank, Japan, and Mexico itself. For the first time, the IMF and the World Bank agreed to offer resources to back debt reduction programs for countries with viable economic programs.

Next we had to work out the "term sheet," or the legal document to support it all. I returned to New York with the lead Mexican negotiator, Angel Gurría, and the rest of the Mexico Advisory Committee. It took until August and went on for 300 pages.

With the new options, the Brady plan provided debtor countries with more debt management flexibility and creditor banks with options that included extending new money on new terms or taking debt reduction instruments that could be traded, thereby overcoming the disadvantage of the illiquidity of previous loans. This started a positive cycle by attracting a wider range of investors, significantly expanding the secondary market and leading to further loan securitization.

Once Mexico's Brady term sheet was finalized, we still had to go around deal by deal. Selling this plan to the banking community was pivotal. Bankers were very hesitant. It's much easier to give an interest-rate cut and get the principal repaid than to acknowledge that part of the principal is not going to be repaid. The amount of zero coupon bonds that the Treasury was willing to issue had a finite limit, so banks became concerned that there would not be enough collateral to cover all of the discount and par bonds that would be issued. Still, we persevered. Immediately after hammering out the legal documents with Angel Gurría in September, I caught the last flight of the day to Paris out of JFK airport to persuade European banks to participate.

The Mexican debt package was signed in February 1990, almost a year after those riots in Venezuela. In the end, 465 of Mexico's 470 creditor banks signed on. The package included most of the debt reduction techniques used previously, such as debt-to-equity conversion, interest-rate reduction, and principal reduction bonds. It also incorporated many of the new money techniques, including bonds, trade finance, and on-lending facilities. In addition, the package included two new techniques: collateralized interest for debt reduction bonds, and value recovery. These two innovations were incorporated into other packages, ultimately including Venezuela's as well. Approximately $44 billion of Mexico's commercial bank debt was converted into bonds on March 28, and as I noted at the time, the transaction was the largest long-term bond issue ever.

The strategy was successful. The debt problem no longer appeared to be a systemic risk. Following Mexico's lead, Brady bond packages substantially reduced debt for Brazil, the Philippines, Costa Rica, Morocco, Chile, Argentina, and Uruguay, among other countries.

Some suggested that this could have been done earlier. However, at the height of the Latin American debt crisis in 1982, banks did not have sufficient capital or reserves to cover the asset write-downs that were required for significant debt reduction. By 1989—following Citibank's huge loss reserves and the follow-on effect in the rest of the banking community in 1987—we had increased our capital and reserves sufficiently to make the Brady plan possible.

Also, debtor countries had not begun to implement basic structural reforms until the mid-1980s. Previous reforms had consisted of a variety of short-term stabilization programs based on adjusting the exchange rate in an attempt to build trade surpluses, which did not address the countries' fundamental economic problems. When banks had tried to prime the pump for reform in Argentina by lending money in advance, it had actually exacerbated the problems.

In Brazil, it was using the Brady plan to restructure the country's outstanding debt that was an important factor contributing to the dramatic resurgence of its economy, which ultimately became resilient enough to weather the crisis of 2008–2009. Brazil wasn't hit as severely as other countries, nor did its downturn last as long.

In large measure, this was due to strong fiscal policies to end hyperinflation, balance the budget, and stabilize the economy, which started to be put into place in 1993 by Fernando Henrique Cardoso, the then finance minister, who later became president on the strength of Brazil's economic turnaround. At the time he was appointed finance minister, in May 1993, Brazil had an annual inflation rate of over 3,000 percent, and a succession of three finance ministers in seven months had tried to bring it under control. The country's economic problems were exacerbated by Brazil's having declared a moratorium on paying its foreign debt obligations in 1987.

This, obviously, had caused a lack of confidence among both the international banking and financial community and the business community, depriving Brazil of the capital it needed to finance growth. Foreign lending to Brazil's steel, retail trade, auto parts, utilities, and telecommunications sectors, among others, had been halted, and runaway inflation had stalled domestic lending as well.

Cardoso was visiting the United Nations in New York in his capacity as foreign minister when President Itamar Franco named him finance minister. When I heard, I made an appointment to meet Cardoso for coffee at the residence of Brazil's ambassador to the United Nations. As the chairman of the bank advisory committee that represented Brazil's 750 foreign creditors, I told him that the Brady plan, already concluded and enacted by Mexico, offered Brazil the best chance it could ever have to restructure its debt, end the overhang from the previous moratorium, and return Brazil to financial stability.

Negotiations, which had begun in 1991, had not been easy. Unlike other countries restructuring under the Brady plan, Brazil chose not to request a special issue of U.S. Treasuries to collateralize its Brady bonds, in part because of the country's precarious foreign currency reserve position. Shortly before the planned announcement of an agreement on the 1992 financing plan, Brazil informed the chairman of the Bank Advisory Committee that it would not have sufficient reserves to purchase U.S. Treasuries to fully collateralize its Brady bonds. Literally overnight, the chair and a small group of the Bank Advisory Committee banks crafted an innovative but complex "phase-in option" for Brazil's collateral requirements and reached agreement with Brazil, which was announced in December 1992.

However, in spite of this announcement, the implementation of the plan had not been concluded when I met with Cardoso in New York. In part, the plan was still bogged down in May 1993 because of several changes in the Finance Ministry during that time.

On several more occasions, including at the IMF–World Bank meetings in Washington, D.C., I emphasized the importance of moving ahead speedily in order to conclude the restructuring, and Cardoso agreed, reviving the discussions with the Bank Advisory Committee. He appointed Pedro Malan, the then executive director at the World Bank, as Brazil's representative on the restructuring committee, with Arminio Fraga (who in later years would be asked to run Brazil's central bank) as Malan's deputy.

By November 1993 we had reached agreement to restructure the $47.3 billion obligation. We all flew to Toronto for a November 29 signing ceremony, giving Brazil an additional five months, until April 15, to implement the conditions for the agreement. The agreement cut Brazil's outstanding debt by about $4 billion and reduced the interest it owed by another $4 billion.

Cardoso wasted no time. He and his government announced the Real plan as soon as Brazil's representatives returned from the signing ceremony, on December 3. He couldn't have announced that plan unless he had gotten the parameters of the debt situation worked out. Getting the debt deal done was clearly a critical move.

Finalization of the debt restructuring was the first step in the recovery as the banks regained confidence and the money started flowing in. The stock market rose 113 percent in 1993 on the strength of Cardoso's reforms and the restoration of confidence of the international banking community. The Real plan, in addition to creating a new currency, put in place structural reforms such as a privatization process, appropriate deregulation, trade liberalization, and tax changes. Importantly, completion of the debt deal and implementation of the Real plan were prerequisites to Cardoso's ability to declare his candidacy for president, the deadline for which was April 2 for an October election. Any delay in the transaction would have jeopardized his aspirations. Indeed, on March 17, 1994, I met Cardoso for coffee at the InterContinental Hotel in New York to iron out the final details associated with the debt exchange. At that meeting, he mentioned his plans to run for president and said that he had taken this trip to New York to discuss with his wife the decision to enter the election. Cardoso was subsequently elected president in October 1994, and he appointed Malan as his own finance minister to continue his program of economic reform to sustain the Real plan, laying the groundwork for Brazil's economic growth and stability today.

The Brady plan was a turning point. The securitization of debt set the tone for the huge flow of private-sector funds into emerging markets. Today, commercial banks are no longer the main holders of emerging-market debt, as they were back in the debt crises of the 1980s. These days, the group of creditors is more diverse, including hedge funds, mutual funds, and pension funds.

Countries that once had no access to capital markets are now able to raise billions. That couldn't have happened without a change in the process—an innovative way of thinking about it, and the persistence to carry it out.

———

IT'S RARE THAT ONE man or woman can carry out a major achievement alone. That's why building consensus is important to the process. Getting all stakeholders to play a role in the solution by giving them a voice in the process is an important way of accomplishing this. It helps also to be able to look at old problems in new ways, putting a new twist or emphasis on what has been tried before and looking to innovative problem solving to adapt to the issue at hand. Team building, consensus building, and innovative solutions are the keys to success.

BIBLIOGRAPHY

TURKEY

Encyclopedia of the Nations. Advameg Inc. http://www.nations encyclopedia.com/Asia-and-Oceania/Turkey-ECONOMY .html, accessed August 13, 2009.

"IMF Set to Approve $10bn for Turkey." *BBC News*, May 15, 2001.

Suskind, Ron. *The Price of Loyalty: George W. Bush, the White House and the Education of Paul O'Neill.* New York: Simon & Schuster, 2004, pp. 173–175.

Taylor, John B. *Global Financial Warriors: The Untold Story of International Finance in the Post-9/11 World.* New York: W. W. Norton, 2007, pp. 167–170.

COMMITTEES AND SUBCOMMITTEES

Boughton, James M. *Silent Revolution: The International Monetary Fund, 1979–1989.* Washington, D.C.: International Monetary Fund, 2001, pp. 364–365.

———

Chernow, Ron. *The House of Morgan: An American Banking Dynasty and the Rise of Modern Finance.* New York: Grove Press, 1990, p. 646.

Ipsen, Erik. "The Eclipse of Advisory Committees." *Institutional Investor,* September 1989, pp. 294–300.

Osborn, Neil. "The Rhodes Show Goes On and On." *Euromoney,* March 1984, pp. 33–37.

Tinn, David B. "The War among Brazil's Bankers." *Fortune,* July 11, 1983, pp. 4–9.

BRADY BONDS

Cline, William R. *International Debt Reexamined.* Washington, D.C.: Institute for International Economics, 1995, pp. 216–319.

Glynn, Lenny. "Taking the Hit on LDC Debt." *Institutional Investor,* July 1987.

Johnston, Moira. *Roller Coaster: The Bank of America and the Future of American Banking.* New York: Ticknor and Fields, 1990, pp. 390–393.

Kilborn, Peter T. "Bush Backs U.S. Shift on World Debt." *New York Times,* December 20, 1988.

Rhodes, William R. "LDC Debt Policy." In Martin Feldstein (ed.) *American Economic Policy in the 1980s.* Chicago and London: University of Chicago Press, 1994, pp. 725–732.

POSTSCRIPT

This book contains many of the lessons that have been fundamental for me in managing the various international financial crises that I have been involved with over the past half century. The events of 2008 to 2009, now termed the Great Recession, and the destabilizing problems experienced by Greece, southern Europe, and Ireland clearly demonstrate that financial crises will continue to occur. Still, the lessons of the last 50 years show that all crises are manageable. I want to underline some of the themes that these situations have in common, with the hope that policymakers will keep them in mind as they attempt to minimize the negative effects a crisis can bring.

Each country is unique, and a cookie-cutter approach does not work when dealing with a nation in crisis. Every country has distinct reasons for why it got into trouble, for how the problems could have been prevented, and for how the crisis could have been resolved. Having said that, there is at least one very important common denominator to be found when looking at sovereign crises around the world; it is the possibility of what is called contagion—a rapid spread of problems from one country to another. The international financial community experienced the dangers of contagion during the crises that enveloped Latin America in the 1980s, Asia in the late 1990s, and later in Europe.

Therefore, we must not lose sight of the risks and speed of contagion, and we should always be mindful of how rapidly markets move.

When facing an economic crisis, the clock is always running against policymakers, so they must act rapidly to implement the necessary reforms and programs to avoid further deterioration. Examples of such measures would include but not be limited to privatizations, trade liberalization, tax reforms, smart regulation, development of a viable domestic capital market and, very importantly, institution building. Experience has taught that time is the enemy. The longer one waits, the more difficult it is to stem the tide, and the ensuing increase in losses will cause the country and its people, along with its bondholders and other creditors, to suffer.

It is vital for a sovereign in trouble to immediately implement reforms and measures that are bold in nature, and as these will deeply impact the country's citizens, it is imperative that a government be able to present the reform program as one of "national" origin in order to avoid the perception that it was imposed, rather than supported, by an outside source, whether it be the IMF or another political or international financial institution. There will be more willingness to accept tough measures when a society understands that those measures are in the country's long-run interest and have been developed domestically. This was the approach that Turkey took in 2001, and it worked well for the country.

Strong political leadership is also essential for a government to carry forward the necessary reforms in a rigorous and timely fashion, as the implementation of these reforms is often very difficult and requires firm management.

And very importantly, the private sector—be it banks, institutional bondholders, or individual bondholders— must be involved in any country reform program from the beginning. In most cases, it holds the majority of the debt and can ultimately help the country return to the capital markets with access to financing at reasonable rates. In my experience, consultation (at a minimum) between public and private sectors has always yielded the best outcome.

Like the ancient Maya, who conceived of time as a series of cycles, we would do well to link the cycles of the present to those of both the past and the future. That means that the lessons derived from experience in the past are relevant not just for the fleeting moments for which they originated but also for what is to come. I am not a fortune teller, but I am an optimist. The world will continue to undergo financial crises again and again, long after I no longer walk this earth. My recommendation is that we try to learn from these experiences and at the same time plan for success, because failure can pretty well take care of itself.

INDEX

ABOUT THE AUTHOR

 Bill Rhodes is President and CEO of William R. Rhodes Global Advisors, LLC, and professor-at-large at Brown University. He is also a senior advisor for Citi, having stepped back from full-time responsibilities after more than 53 years with the institution. He is the retired senior vice chairman and senior international officer of Citigroup and Citibank.

Mr. Rhodes gained a reputation for international financial diplomacy in the 1980s as a result of his leadership in helping manage the external debt crises that involved developing nations and their creditors worldwide. During that period and in the 1990s, he headed the advisory committees of international banks that negotiated debt-restructuring agreements for Argentina, Brazil, Jamaica, Mexico, Peru, and Uruguay. In 1998, when the Republic of South Korea experienced liquidity problems, he chaired the international bank group that negotiated the extension of short-term debt of the South Korean banking system. In early 1999, at the request of the government of Brazil, he acted as worldwide coordinator to help implement the maintenance of trade and interbank lines by foreign commercial banks to Brazil. He has since served as a trusted advisor to governments, financial officials, and corporations worldwide.

Mr. Rhodes is a director of the Private Export Funding Corporation; a senior advisor to the World Economic Forum; chairman of the U.S.-Korea Business Council; vice chairman of the National Committee on U.S.- China Relations; a director of the U.S.–Hong Kong Business Council; a director of the Korea Society; a director of the U.S.-China Business Council; a member of South Korean president Lee's Council of Global Advisors; a member of the International Advisory Board of the National Bank of Kuwait; a senior advisor to the Dalian Government in China; a member of the Inter-American Development Bank's Private Sector Advisory Board; a member of the International Policy Committee of the U.S. Chamber of Commerce; a member of the board at the Foreign Policy Association; a trustee of the Asia Society; and a trustee of the Economic Club of New York. He is also a member of the U.S.-Brazil CEO Forum and a member of the Advisory Council of the Brazilian American Chamber of Commerce, the Council on Foreign Relations, and The Group of Thirty. He is a first vice chairman emeritus of the Institute of International Finance and chairman emeritus of the Americas Society and Council of the Americas. He previously served as chairman of the New York Blood Center and the Bankers Association for Finance and Trade.

Mr. Rhodes is a governor and trustee of The New York-Presbyterian Hospital; a member of the Lincoln Center Consolidated Corporate Fund Leadership Committee; a member of the Metropolitan Museum of Art Business Committee and Chairman's Committee; and chairman emeritus of the Board of Trustees of the Northfield Mount Hermon School.

He has received decorations and honors from various governments and institutions, including an honorary doctorate in humane letters from his alma mater, Brown University, where he established the William R. Rhodes Center for International Economics and Finance; Chevalier and Officer of France's Legion of Honor; decorations from Poland, South Korea, Brazil, Mexico, Argentina, Venezuela, Colombia, Panama, and Jamaica; and multiple awards from not-for-profit organizations such as the Africa-America Institute and the Arab Bankers Association of North America in recognition of his contributions to international banking and finance.